VILLAGES OF FIFE

RAYMOND LAMONT-BROWN

D1388272

JOHN DONALD PUBLISHERS
EDINBURGH

First published in 2002
by John Donald Publishers
an imprint of Birlinn Ltd
West Newington House
10 Newington Road
Edinburgh
EH9 1QS

www.birlinn.co.uk

ISBN 0 85976 572 5

British Library Cataloguing-in-Publication Data
A catalogue record for this book is available
from the British Library

Typeset by Koinonia, Manchester
Printed and bound by Antony Rowe Ltd, Chippenham

CONTENTS

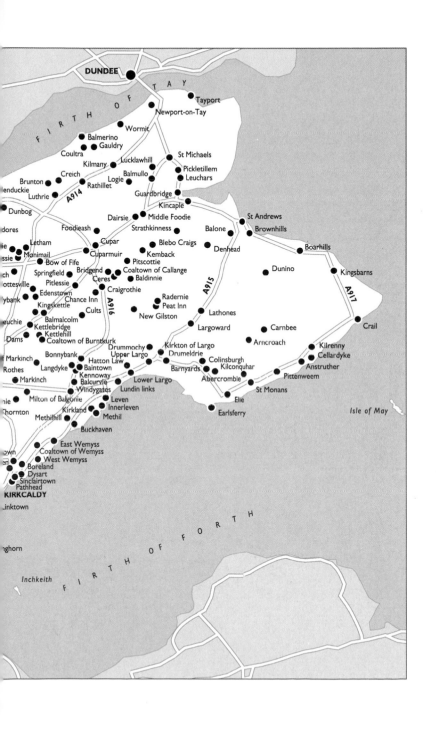

ACKNOWLEDGEMENTS

Many miles have been undertaken across Fife to produce this book. Many conversations have been enjoyed with Fifers keen to recount their village stories – too many names to mention here. But to all a grateful thanks. A special thanks, too, goes to my wife Dr Moira Lamont-Brown, for her companionship in covering Fife from east to west and back again.

In terms of seeking research sources, I would like to thank the following: Dr Simon Taylor of the School of History, Department of Medieval History, University of St Andrews, for his sage advice on Fife village and place names; the staff of the Fife Council East Area Library HQ, Cupar; the staff of the Planning and Building Control Department, Fife Council; Fife Council Chief Executive's Service; and the staff of the public library reference departments at Kirkcaldy and Dunfermline.

The opinions expressed in the volume are my own based on original research in private and public collections. Historians born and unborn will expand, cavil at and pore over extant Fife village histories, but hopefully their updates will be based on honest, impartial research. If this book has done anything to encourage this, or tempt Fife folk and their friends elsewhere to delve into the county's village histories, then I will be rewarded.

THE MAKING OF FIFE'S VILLAGES

TOWARDS A DEFINITION

What is a village? Here is a competent dictionary definition: 'an assemblage of houses smaller than a town'.* This book aims to be a little less rigid than that to include the ever expanding Fife 'small towns' to evoke their village beginnings. Thus the reader should not be surprised to see included such places as Crail, which though created a royal burgh in 1310, and undoubtedly a 'toun' in historical development, retains for the local and outsider alike a village heart with parish church, tolbooth and marketplace – the site of a medieval mercat known from Scandinavia to Brittany as one of the best in Europe.

The landscape of modern Fife is the inheritance left by generations of Fifers' activities, and the building block of Fife's bustling towns was the hamlet and village. The modern facets of Fife's villages reveal clues of a multi-tiered story of change. When Fife emerged from prehistoric clan groupings, say by the fifth century, its inhabitants lived in scattered farmsteads and hamlets, some of short duration – for most dwellings were of flimsy construction and had to be rebuilt every generation or so. In time a pattern of villages appeared in Fife with two maternal roots.

First, castles, abbeys and priories produced dependent hamlets, which developed into villages, then towns, some as burghs of barony, regality or royal burghs. A burgh of barony was under the jurisdiction of a baron or senior cleric, with mandate directly from the Crown; a burgh of regality was under the jurisdiction of a Lord of Regality, a privilege granted by the sovereign; while a royal burgh was considered the 'monarch's own'. The second village root was the ferm-toun, to supply the needs of agriculture. As the supply of services to the rural population multiplied beyond farm boundaries, hamlets and villages developed, with some as 'planned villages' by local landowners. Some villages evolved as habitations of a variety of craftsmen from weavers to wrights, and from shoemakers to farriers.

* Fife Council define a hamlet as being a settlement without a church; a population of 100 constitutes a settlement, and under 3,000 a village.

VILLAGES EVOLVE

Once Fife sported a whole range of 'classic villages'. Each was a complete settlement with parish kirk and incumbent minister, a school with resident schoolmaster, a shop – probably a 'jenny-a'-thing' which sold a multitude of wares – an inn or two, and a 'big hoose' for gentry in its own policies. Today the structure has changed; the kirk still stands, but the minister may serve two or more parishes, and the manse is likely to have been sold off to incomers who retain the name 'The Old Manse', or 'Old Rectory' if the parish had an Episcopalian church. Many of Fife's villages had a railway station, and some hamlets a 'halt'; most of these routes were axed in the 1950s and 1960s, but several station buildings have become private dwellings with sidings as gardens.

A hundred years ago the county directories showed the patterns of Fife village population: a class system in itself. At the apex were the landowners, titled and untitled, then the assortment of eminent personages of the parish, a whole army of artisans from flaxdressers, ratcatchers and millers, to masons, coopers and bakers, with a lower layer of the poor. The latter were often supported by church door alms, and other funds distributed by local Kirk Sessions and trusts set up by philanthropists. Today Fife's village populations have been diluted by incomers who work elsewhere and have their roots far from the old parish boundaries.

Most of Fife's villages and hamlets existed long before written records came into being, and quite often place names of archaic type are all that we have to go on as to when a habitation might have begun. The structure of Fife's villages, too, depend on their history and ownership. Some are simply 'roadside villages', ribboned along one main street; others grouped round a green, more set out at the whim of a landowner; while others conform to no set plan where land might have been designated as 'common' wherein people squatted.

From the 1760s Scotland's Industrial Revolution also contributed to village development, with hamlets local to towns being absorbed into the new burgh boundaries and thus losing their individuality. Perhaps it would be true to say that the golden age of the Fife village was the 1850s, for after that came decades of decline with depression in farming, the collapse of mining and the vanishing of the weaving trade.

Yet even at its apogee, life in Fife villages was rarely sublime, for most of Fife villagers endured a lifetime of poverty and a hardship of weather and finance little understood today.

Because of the important place in the kingdom of Scotland held by Fife after the regal reforms of the eleventh and twelfth centuries the region's villages were never isolated like other Scots rural communities. With St Andrews as the ecclesiastical capital of Scotland and the hunting forests of Fife a magnet for royal activity, the medieval Fife village saw the passage of the good and the great as commonplace. And because of Fife's importance as a source of agricultural products, fishing and mineral resources Fife's towns and villages held a key position in the Scots economy.

The buildings within Fife's villages evolved from local traditions and conditions; few houses reflected an architect's hand and most depended upon the needs, finances and materials available to the communities. Because of transportation costs, the buildings in early Fife villages were made of the materials near at hand. As Fife possessed much good woodland many early village houses were timber framed, and many medieval village houses were thatched with reeds or heather. When serviceable stone was available it was quarried, but many houses were made of field stone (chunks lying on the land), or that washed down by flood. The key buildings in a village constructed of properly treated ashlar were the church, the manse and the mansion house. These were followed by inns, schools, village halls and mill houses.

'MONASTIC' VILLAGES

Many of Fife's hamlets and villages were founded by monastic houses where the secular inhabitants worked for the religious houses on granges, in mines or undertook parish duties. This was true also of monastic landlords in settlements that developed into Fife's burghs. One group in particular were prominent Fife landowners whose order gave its name to lands and areas; the use of the word 'Temple' in place names (such as Lower Largo) remembers the Knights Templars.

The Order of the Knights Templars, like the Knights Hospitallers, originated in the Holy Land. Following the fall of the Holy City of Jerusalem into the hands of Caliph Omar in 636, the reality that Muslims controlled the Christian-associated holy places rankled with the developing medieval church. In 1023 certain merchants from Amalfi, Italy, obtained permission from the Caliph of Egypt to establish a hospice for Christian pilgrims to the holy sites, and from this was established the famous Order of the Knights of St John of Jerusalem. When Godfrey de Bouillon took Jerusalem for the Christians in the First Crusade (1096), his wounded soldiers were treated by the organisation set up by the Amalfi merchants, and in the eight military crusades thereafter the hospitallers played their part.

It is said that the Knights Templars were introduced into Scotland by David I around 1128–53, organised from a base at Balantrodoch, Midlothian and Maryculter, Kincardine; the Knights Hospitallers had their headquarters at Torphichen. The Knights Templars, with their distinctive habit of white mantle with red cross, had their headquarters at the palace of the Latin Knights of Jerusalem at Mount Moriah within the Temple area. Their special tasks were to guard the routes to Jerusalem and assist pilgrims visiting the holy places. In time they began to be very rich landowners through secular bequests and property gifts. Fife played a prominent role in this with important Templar possessions in the following fourteen village/burgh locations:

Aberdour	Inverkeithing
Anstruther Easter	Kinghorn
Anstruther Wester	Kirkcaldy
Burntisland	Leslie
Crail	Pittencrieff
Cupar	St Andrews
Dunfermline	Strathmiglo

The following religious landlords played an important role in the history of Fife hamlets and villages as their monastic records show:

Benedictines:	Dunfermline Priory/Abbey
	Isle of May Priory
Order of Tiron:	Lindores Abbey
Cistercians:	Balmerino Abbey
	Gadvan Preceptory
Augustinians:	Pittenweem Priory
	Portmoak (St Serf's, Lochleven) – now outside Fife
Dominican friars:	St Katherine's, Cupar

St Monan's, St Monans
Assumption and Coronation of the Blessed
Virgin, St Andrews

Franciscans:
Aberdour (nuns)
Crail (nuns)
Inverkeithing
St Andrews

Secular canons/colleges: Crail
St Andrews

Note: Crawford Priory, Cupar and Inchyra Abbey, Newburgh, are fanciful
nineteenth-century names.

VILLAGES AND EPONYMOUS PARISHES

By the reign of William I, the Lion (1165–1214), Fife villages were
divided into fifty-one parishes which were to remain intact until the
Reformation of 1558–60. From the charters of William I they may be
listed thus in source spellings:

In the Deanery of Forthrif

*Ecclesia de Clackmannan	Auchtermuchty	Kemback
*De Muckard	Arngosk	Dinnino
Karnock	Forther	St Andrews
Torry	Quilt	
Dunfermling	Lathrisk cum capella	

Arch-deanery of St Andrews

Innerkeithing	Leuchars cum capella	Kinghorn
Kircaldie	Dysart	Weems
Methil	*Cleish	*Kinross
*Portmoke	Kinglassie	Markinch
Auchterdiran cum capel	Wester Kinghorn or Burntisland	

In Deanery of Fife

Forgund	Ecclesia de Carale	Logy-Murdo
Kilrinny	Kilmany	Anstruther
Flisk cum capella	Abercrumby	Lundoris
Kilconquhar cum capella	Kelly	Cullessie
Monymeal	Newburn	Largo
Creich cum capella	Dunbog	Scoony
Cupar	Kennoway	Moonsy
Siras	Darsy	Tarvet

Parishes marked * are no longer in Fife.

Fife had two types of parish. *Quod sacra* parishes were those with functions that were ecclesiastical only and were created by statute when an old parish became too large for a single minister to tend. *Quod omnia* parishes combined secular and ecclesiastical roles. In time the parishes lost their civil administrative duties, that is regarding villages, when civil matters were transferred to other local government bodies. From 1840 the Fife parishes had been expanded to sixty-one on the medieval model to be listed thus:

Cupar Presbytery
Abdie Strathmiglo
Auchtermuchty
Balmerino
Ceres
Collessie
Criech
Cults
Cupar
Dairsie
Dunbog
Falkland
Flisk
Kettle
Kilmany
Logie
Monimail
Moonzie
Newburgh

St Andrews Presbytery
Abercrombie/St Monance
Anstruther Easter/Wester
Cameron
Carnbee
Crail
Denino
Elie
Ferryport-on-Craig
Forgan, or St Fillans
Kemback
Kilconquhar
Kilrenny
Kingsbarns
Largo
Leuchars
Newburgh
Pittenweem
St Andrews St Leonards

Kirkcaldy Presbytery
Abbotshall
Auchterderran
Auchtertool
Ballingray
Burntisland
Dysart
Kennoway
Kinghorn
Kinglassie
Kirkcaldy
Leslie
Markinch
Scoonie, or Leven
Wemyss

Dunfermline Presbytery
Aberdour
Beath
Carnock
Dalgetty
Dunfermline
Inverkeithing
Saline
Torryburn

Today the villages of Fife are set out in these parishes by the Church of Scotland as clergy 'charges'. It is interesting to compare them with their medieval forerunners:

Presbytery of Kirkcaldy	*Presbytery of St Andrews*
Auchterderran, with Kinglassie and Cardenden	Abdie, with Dunbog and Newburgh
St Fothad's	Anstruther
Auchtertool with Kirkcaldy	Auchtermuchty
Linktown	Balmerino with Wormit
Buckhaven	Boarhills with Dunino
Burntisland	Cameron
Denbeath with Methilhill	Carnbee with Pittenweem
Dysart	Cellardyke with Kilrenny
Glenrothes	Ceres with Springfield
Innerleven East	Crail with Kingsbarns
Kennoway	Creich, Flisk and Kilmany with Monimail
Kinghorn with Kirkcaldy	Cupar
Leslie Trinity	Dairsie, Kemback with Strathkinness
Leven	Edenshead and Strathmiglo
Markinch	Elie, Kilconquhar with Colinsburgh
Methil	Falkland with Freuchie
Thornton	Howe of Fife
Wemyss	Largo and Newburn with Largo St Davids
Windygates and Balgonie	Largoward with St Monans
	Leuchars with Guardbridge
	Newport on Tay
	St Andrews
	St Leonards with Cameron
	Tayport

VILLAGE FOLK

From the development of Fife village society three personages were to play prominent leadership roles: the laird, the minister and the schoolmaster, though by the nineteenth century they were joined by the local doctor. These men had the most regular contact with village folk; county administrators like the lord-lieutenant, the sheriff-depute and the members of parliament were distant figures both socially and functionally.

To a large extent up to the late nineteenth century Fife gentry were absentee land proprietors. They looked to England for their education and prosperity: after all from 1603 and 1707 in particular

the glittering economic prizes, court privileges and political advance-
ment were all to be found in London. With some few exceptions Fife
gentry were a breed apart from village folk.

Fife lairds came in for an amount of ridicule. The fine folk of
Edinburgh, for instance, said they could identify a Fife laird by the
salt water on his hat; an allusion to the often choppy crossing of the
Forth to the 'civilisation' of the capital. There's many a proverb too
about Fife lairds; one of the most representative is:

Aye daft and maistly drunk, and what they want in sense they have in greed.

The Scottish ballad writer Caroline, Baroness Nairne (1766–1845)
made a play on this proverb in one of her songs:

Ye shouldna ca' the Laird daft, tho' daft-like he may be;
Ye shouldna ca' the Laird daft, he's just as wise as we;
Ye shouldna ca' the Laird daft, his bonnet has a bee;
He's just a wee bit Fifish, like some Fife Lairds that be.

Who knew the villagers best? Undoubtedly the inhabitants of the
manse and the schoolhouse. The central building in almost every Fife
village is its parish church. Whether or not it is redundant now, it was
essential to past community life for centuries. The church remains
the most history-absorbed artefact in Fife's village communities even
though its purpose is often deemed irrelevant to those who now
dwell in its shadow.

Fife's village churches run the gamut of ecclesiastical history;
some were built in the Middle Ages; some were constructed on sites
of pagan worship; some developed from the presence of a saint's
relic; and to many some of Scotland's great missionaries like the Rev.
Thomas Chalmers of Kilmany may have drawn crowds.

The immediate environs of the village church, its graveyard, is the
place to find out about any village ancestors. Here lie the old families
of the area, and individuals who were the heart of the local community for as long as the village existed. As many of Fife's pre-
Reformation churches have been rebuilt or remodelled a historical
survey has to include looking for fragments in walls and pavements
for the village's Pictish origins, say, or medieval glory. Village folk in
Fife were always thrifty in recycling fine stone be it granite tomb-
stones for paths or prehistoric sarcens to prop up a tower.

By the eighteenth century ministers ceased to be of the same social
class as the landed gentry, although most in Fife depended on the
Crown for patronage or on the landed heritors with whom they

were often in dispute regarding stipends and church provisions. Still by the beginning of the twentieth century Fife village life centred largely on the church, with ministers often remaining in their parishes for decades.

Because of his social position the minister was a man of consequence in Fife villages; a superior education made him a mentor whose advice was sought on a range of matters spiritual and temporal. He acted as welfare officer, marriage guidance counsellor, community poor-fund organiser and burial-ground director. As Dr Wilson R. McNair commented in his *Doctor's Progress*:

> Ministers formed a class all by themselves, and were a constant source of interest and discussion. Everybody sat 'under' one or other of them, and it was a point of honour to uphold your choice as the finest preacher in the country. The sermons were long and, usually, insufferably tedious. So much so, indeed, that the jokes fired off at Church social gatherings were often, in reality, backhanders at the minister.

When a village church pulpit became vacant the community often excited itself into a fever to match a heated parliamentary election. Kirk elders would go forth to hear other ministers preach, or invite ministers to preach in their own territory. Then a round of communicants' votes were taken with the successful candidate being 'called' to the vacancy.

Because of their intimate knowledge of the private lives of village folk, ministers were a fount of information about the character of the people they ministered to. Writing in the 1790s the Rev. Alexander Brodie of Carnbee had this to say about his flock's strengths and weaknesses:

> They are in general a sober and industrious people, religiously disposed, and mind their own affairs. In the last age, when smuggling was carried to a great length in this neighbourhood, many of the farmers and others were, by various means, induced to give assistance to the smugglers, in carrying away and disposing of vast quantities of foreign spirits, which had a very bad effect upon their health and morals. Happily, however, that illicit trade is now in great measure abandoned, and the farmers, with their servants, now employ themselves to much better purpose in proving their lands.

Many villages produced their own idiosyncratic atmosphere because of the nature of the predominant craft or employment. Thus the weavers of, say, Dura Den or Kingskettle, were different from the miners of Torryburn. Here is what the Rev. Andrew Bell had to say about his parishioners at Crail:

The credulity of former times with respect to witches is almost extinguished, and the little superstitious fancies, which so frequently prevail among the commonalty, are gradually losing ground. The practice of innoculating for the small-pox has been much retarded, partly by religious scruples, and partly by the expense of medical aid. To the cleanness and commodiousness of their habitations, they are beginning to pay greater attention than formerly. When dressed they are decently neat, rather than fine. If they are not remarkable for sobriety and industry, neither do they deserve to be stigmatised as dissipated and idle. Their ideas and sentiments are gradually acquiring a greater degree of liberality. The ordinances of religion are respected, a tolerable decorum of manners is observed, though here there are exceptions as well as in every numerous society; as subjects they are peaceable and loyal, and by no means fond of 'meddling with those who are given to change'.

Among the Rev. Bell's contemporaries, the Rev. Peter Primrose noted that the miners of Dalgety were becoming more 'civilised', while schoolmaster William West of Dunino noted that his neighbours of the 'inferior classes' were 'uncommonly fond of personal decoration'. At Inverkeithing the Rev. Andrew Robertson sighed that 'Burgh politics, and the election of members of parliament, have an unhappy influence upon the morals of the people' – he noted that there was great 'animosity' between opposing candidates' supporters at election time that kept people from their religious devotions. Overall though, the Rev. James McDonald of Kemback summed up what most eighteenth-century ministers thought of their Fife villagers: 'In general, they are sober minded, industrious, and temperate; decent in their manners, attending to their own business, living in peace with one another, and giving regular attendance upon the public ordinances of religion.' The Rev. McDonald went on to note: 'During the incumbency of the present minister, which comprehends a period of nearly thirteen years, there has not occurred a single instance of any person belonging to this parish suffering the slightest punishment from a civil judge.'

Thus in the eighteenth and nineteenth centuries, in particular, village folk were deemed law abiding. Commissioner Hill of the Scottish Prisons Inspectorate confirmed this in his report of 1840 when he wrote: 'There is but little crime at present in Fifeshire'. Those who erred, he recorded, were mostly between twelve and thirty and the most common crimes were assault and petty theft. Farm servants, he concluded, were few among the lists of offenders, who seemed to be mostly vagrants and opportunist thieves, and assaults were the result mostly of drunkenness. Village folk, then, were a peace-loving community.

Often the Fife village school is found in the shadow of the church, or some other central position, integral to the main street to blend with cottages and shops. Most of Fife's extant village schools are of Victorian or Edwardian date, and although some are now converted into private houses, they often remain a part of community life for meetings, social events and the like. As with his school, or the local manse, the schoolmaster's house has frequently been sold off.

Fife's village schools were regulated by the Act of 1696 by which heritors had to supply a schoolhouse and fund a schoolmaster's salary. By the Education (Scotland) Act of 1872, the state for the first time became directly responsible for educating children. Even so village school boards were charged with the administration and set the rate at which parents would pay for their children's education. The usual fee around the time of the Act was 2d (1p) per week, but the Education Act of 1890 made education virtually free.

Local history was often an interest of both minister and schoolmaster, and the records we can now access of early Fife village life were the work of these men, who were often joined in their labours by the local doctor. General practitioners came late on the historical scene, village medical needs being supplied by quack or competent apothecaries, local women skilled in commonsense cures for minor ailments and hospital physicians and surgeons. After the Medical Act of 1858 recognised doctors as a professional group, general practitioner practices slowly began to be set up in villages. All was to change again with the coming of the National Health Service (Scotland) Bill in 1948.

Fife village folk turn up in several Scots ballads and songs; often they were associated with musical instruments. Burns evokes his 'piper out o' Fife' while the comic tune 'There cam' a Fiddler out o' Fife' mentions another. Trades too are represented as in 'There was a wee Cooper that lived in Fife'. A popular song to recite or sing at Victorian musical evenings was simply called the 'Auld Scots Burgh'. It's probably meant to represent Anstruther, but it could fit a multitude of Fife locations.

> In Scotland stands an ancient burgh wi' some twal hundred people,
> A lang and narrow strip o'street and ae high-shouldered steeple;
> Ilk grocer i' the burgh is a baillie or has been,
> But the Provost was perpetual, and drave the hale machine.

At twal o'clock the Provost cam' and stoud upo' the street,
And waggit to his right-hand man i' the public-house to meet;
The baillie threw his apron by, and o'er their gill they sat,
And they managed a' the toun's affairs in a bit quiet Chat.
The Deacon, wi' a face half-washed, gaed consequential by,
But the Deacon as a'body kent had nae finger in the pie:
The Deacon made the Provost's breeks and a' his laddies' claes,
And the Provost, tho' the best o' friends, was yet the warst o' faes.
And when the canvassin' cam' round the member walked about,
And linkit i' the Provost's arm, they sought the Deacon out.
The bodies threw their night-caps by, or wi' them cleared a chair,
And the member sat i' the ben house wi' a condescendin' air.

And so the song lampooned how a few people only ran Fife communities, often from the comfort of an ale-house, while the local MP was only seen at election time.

FIFE SETTLEMENTS, HAMLETS AND VILLAGES THAT BECAME BURGHS

RB: Royal burghs – the town belonged to the monarch.
BR: Burghs of regality – a post-Reformation burgh, holding from a subject of the Crown, sometimes a cleric in holy orders, or a peer of the realm, with some rights to administer justice.
EB: Ecclesiastical burghs – specifically with a clerical superior. With rights as of BR and BB.
BB: Burghs of barony – a late medieval burgh, holding from a subject of the Crown, having limited privileges of manufactures, markets and fairs. Superior usually a member of the influential laity; probably a baron.

Aberdour Wester, BB 1500–01
Anstruther Easter, BB 1571–2, RB 1583
Anstruther Wester, BB 1540–1, RB 1587
Auchtermuchty, RB 1517
Auchtertool, BB 1617
Burntisland, RB 1541
Ceres, BB 1620
Colinsburgh, BB 1707
Crail, RB 1150–52
Culross, BB 1490, RB 1592
Cupar, RB 1327
Dunbog, BB 1687
Dunfermline, EB 1303
Dysart, RB 1594

Earlsferry, EB 1541, RB 1589
Elie, BB 1598–9
Falkland, RB 1458
Ferryport-on-Craig – Tayport, BB 1598–9
Fifeness, BB 1707
Innergelly, BB 1623
Inverkeithing, RB 1341
Kennoway, BB 1663
Kilmany, BB 1578
Kilrenny, RB 1592
Kinghorn, RB 1165–72
Kirkcaldy, EB 1315–28, RB 1644
Largo, BB 1513
Leslie Green, BB 1457–8
Linktown, BB 1663
Markinch, BB 1678
Methil, BB 1662
Newbigging, BB 1541
Newburgh, EB 1266, RB 1631
Pitlessie, BB 1526
Pittenweem, RB 1541
St Andrews, EB 1124–44, RB 1620
St Monans, BB 1596
Strathmiglo, BB 1509–10
Valleyfield, BB 1663
Wemyss, BB 1511

VILLAGE 'CORES': DUNFERMLINE, KIRKCALDY, CUPAR AND ST ANDREWS

The town of Dunfermline, created a royal burgh on 24 May 1588 by James VI, who confirmed in that document all past charters, owed its origin to the environs of the royal palace and monastery, the Christ Church of the latter – a daughter house of Christ Church, Canterbury – having national status as the 'common cemetery of the Kings of Scotland' as Dundee-born Hector Boece (*c.*1465–1536) put it. Even in 1600, with around 1,000 inhabitants, Dunfermline was little more than a village, although by the fifteenth century the manufacture of wool and linen products had made the place thrive. Civically Dunfermline had a mercat cross by 1438, which stood in High St at the junction with Cross Wynd, until it was removed at the opening of Guildhall St, 1752; and a tolbooth by 1433 at the west end of High

A late nineteenth-century sketch of Dunfermline, showing the medieval abbey on the hill, with Pittencrieff Park to the left. Here the core of the hamlet that grew into Dunfermline was situated; Priory Lane in the foreground marks the extent of the medieval enclave. [*Author's collection*]

St (it was removed in 1769); the Tron, or public weight-beam, was by the tolbooth and is first mentioned in 1383.

Tradition has it that King Malcolm III, bynamed Canmore, or 'great head', who was born around 1031, erected a fortified building here from the time he ascended the Scottish throne in 1058. This place became his headquarters and a rather featureless ruin at Tower Hill, above the Tower Burn, is still pointed out as Malcolm Canmore's Tower in Dunfermline's Pittencrieff Park. Here then began the original settlement; this collection of dwellings seems to have declined at the end of the twelfth century when its inhabitants were, probably, absorbed into a new township.

This new township developed with the founding of a priory with a church dedicated to the Holy Trinity, around 1070, by Malcolm's queen, Margaret; this became an abbey complex in 1128, founded by Malcolm and Margaret's third reigning son David I. By this time David was calling the new township *meus burgus*, and after Robert I, the Bruce, came to the throne in 1306, the settlement was dependent upon the abbey; the settlement was a burgh of barony by 1488 to be stented (assessed for taxes) in 1538. Thus the village core of Dunfermline became a suburb of the abbey which was annexed to the Crown in 1593. The fourteenth-century south-western range of the abbey was later used as a palace and continued as a principal

Kirk Wynd, Kirkcaldy in the 1890s. Here the Old Parish Church, with its tower of around 1500, marks where the Middle Ages village first spilled down to the harbour to form the new burgh which engulfed the nearby villages of Sinclairtown, Gallatown, Pathhead and Linktown. [*Staralp*]

residence for Scottish monarchs until the seventeenth century. It is worth noting too, that the settlement (and abbey) were attacked by Edward I in 1303, by Richard II's army in 1385, and suffered when the religious reformers demolished parts of the abbey in 1560, as well as in the fire of 1624. Today the medieval core of Dunfermline can be identified as largely bounded by modern Kirkgate, Canmore St, High St (once Causagait and other names), the main medieval

thoroughfare and New Row, the main medieval route to the Forth,
and as far down as Nethertown Broad Street. Excavation of burgage
plots in the 1990s seem to confirm this core location.

Kirkcaldy evolved as a settlement around 1070, when Malcolm III
gave whatever was extant to the clergy of the church of the Holy
Trinity at Dunfermline; a gift confirmed by his son David I in 1130.
Thus the early village and harbour became a burgh of regality under
the succeeding abbots of Dunfermline until they disponed it in 1450
to the baillies and the commonalty of Kirkcaldy. Charles I ratified all
the gifts of his predecessors by the Act of Parliament of 1644;
Charles II elevated the town into a royal burgh in 1661. Thus the
early village core of Kirkcaldy was by the extant harbour. The coastal
track east-west from the harbour settlement gave a delineation of
how Kirkcaldy was to evolve. The modern town developed from one
street (mirroring the old village track) that ran from Bridgeton and
Morningside, in Inverteil, through Linktown and Kirkcaldy proper,
on to Pathhead, Sinclairtown and Gallatown: this made a four-mile
strip whose associate dwellings gave Kirkcaldy its name of 'The Lang
Toun'.

The earliest document referring to Cupar is dated 28 June 1381,
and is a grant by Robert II to the burgh to have a free port on the
Motray Water. Some historians have suggested though that Cupar
was one of the royal burghs so founded by William I, the Lion, who
was born in 1143 and succeeded Malcolm IV, the Maiden, in 1165,
reigning until 1214. Certainly, Cupar was important enough by 1276
for Alexander III to hold an assembly of nobles here. By the mid-
fifteenth century Cupar had grown rich by a sea trade with Flanders.
Cupar Castle, its site traditionally pointed out at School Hill, was
taken by Edward I in 1296. By 1348 Duncan, Earl of Fife, whose
predecessors probably built the castle, founded the Dominican
Friary of St Katherine at Cupar; these ecclesiastical lands were given
to the burgh by James VI in 1572 thus swelling the original policies
of the village core. Cupar's village core lay on the left bank of the
Eden Water and was bounded in medieval times by Crossgate, with
the Mill Port (Millgate) at its south end, leading into Bonnygate,
with the West Port at its west end, and St Catherine's St, where the
East Port was, with spurs into such as Lady Wynd and a development of ribbon burgages along the West Port.

The settlement that became the city of St Andrews was founded
some time betwen 1140 and 1153 by the diocesan bishop, Robert,

erstwhile prior of the Augustinian foundation at Scone, who held the See until his death in 1159. When Robert founded his burgh, enhanced by the gift of a *vil* of land by David I, there was already a settlement on the nearby triangular headland which was associated, from the eighth century, with the religious enclave of *Kinrimund* ('the head of the king's mount'). During the episcopate of Bishop Richard (1163–78), a charter tells us that the core settlement that became St Andrews was located in the area that is now North and South Castle St, East Scores and the east end of North Street. From this focus, and the precincts of the cathedral, developed the three main streets that would define St Andrews's burgh thoroughfares, *Vicus Borealis* (North Street), *Vicus Australis* (South Street) and *Vicus Fori* (Market Street). The mercat cross (removed 1768) was sited where Market Street meets College Street and Church Street, not far from the now vanished tolbooth (demolished 1862).

On 13 August 1472 the then bishop of St Andrews, Patrick Graham, was advanced by the Bull of Pope Sixtus IV to archbishop and metropolitan (administrative head) of the province which stretched from Aberdeen to the Tweed, confirming St Andrews as a city. St Andrews was confirmed as a royal burgh on 28 February 1620.

North Street, St Andrews, looking west from the Ladyhead. Here the town's fisherfolk had an enclave which formed a village within the medieval town. This turn-of-the-century picture shows the tower of St Salvator's College, *c.* 1550, on the right. [*Alexander B. Paterson*]

PLOTTING VILLAGE HISTORY

Despite the collapse of the rural society to which they owed their development, the essential elements of the Fife village remain – dwellings, public houses, shops, the church and manse, schoolhouse and school and mansion house; though the latter may be ruined, like any medieval castle, its presence probably sponsored a settlement. Along with other relics like abbeys, priories, harbours, doocots and windmills, all this infrastructure supplies a starting place for researching a village history. Where no obvious 'sponsoring' building is extant to trace a village's roots, a nucleus might have been a farmstead, by a spring or good water supply. From this, maps marking field boundaries might help as might the names of fields and the location of barns and plantations, to show how an initial hamlet developed.

Here is a checklist of source subject areas to explore in seeking out village history:

Public and research libraries: local history books; journals; pamphlets; antiquarian/history society proceedings; diaries; newspaper/magazine articles.

Prints and photographs.

Ephemera: village fête programmes; tradesmens' cards; adverts.

Public archives and record offices: Scottish Records Office; National Library of Scotland; National Monuments Records; university archives; government papers; judicial records; church records; social welfare records; education papers.

Sociological studies: property registers.

Private archives: family and estate histories; Employment, Trade Union, Workers' Benefit and Association Records.

Physical geography: topographical maps and plans.

As the Middle Ages developed, Fife was included in the custom which had spread from Europe to preserve transactions of land and property between individuals in documents known as 'instruments'. These records were kept by notaries: so look for Notary Instruments for details of such ownership. Again look for Registers of Sasines (in the General Register at Edinburgh): these give property details from feudal times.

Further, many Fife villages have legends and myths grown from folklore seedcorn in the distant past; many such have become embellished or warped in the telling over the years. The fact that they are often untrue does not detract from their relevance within the society which gave birth to them and no village history has flavour without them.

A starting point for some might be in the assessment of village names. Many of Fife's village names have Pictish or Gaelic roots, some contain the given names of founders while others represent the work environment which caused them to be established. Street names, too, often give vital clues to how a village developed.

Here is a representative sample of Fife village names:

ABERCROMBIE	Pictish *abor* 'river or burn mouth'
ANSTRUTHER	From *sruthair*, 'a place of streams'
ARNCROACH	*Ard* and *cruach*, 'crest of the gallows/hill'
AUCHMUTY	Gaelic *auch* from *ath* 'ford' and *mult* (castrated lamb)
AUCHTERDERRAN	Gaelic *uachdar*, 'upland' and *daire*, 'oakwood'
BALBIRNIE	Gaelic *baile-braon*, 'farm of the damp place'
BINNEND	*Beinn*, 'a peak'
BLEBO CRAIGS	*Bladebolg*, 'crags of the bag-like hill'
BORELAND	Sheltered land, of a feudal superior
BOW OF FIFE	Bend of Fife?
BRUNTON	Suggesting land cleared by fire
CADHAM	*Caldhame*, cold home
CARDENDEN	Gaelic *carden*, 'forest' and *den*, for deep valley
CARNBEE	*Carn* and *binnein*, 'cairn of the peak'
CELLARDYKE	Once Skinfasthaven. Scots *Siller*, 'silver' and *dyke*, 'wall'
CLUNY	*Cloan*, 'a slope', down to a force/bridge
COLLESSIE	*Cul* and *lios*, 'the back of cultivated land'
COULTRA	*Cultrach*, 'rear of the shore'
CRAIGROTHIE	*Craig*, 'rock' and *rath*, 'fort'
CREICH	*Crioch*, 'boundary'
DALGETY BAY	Topographical name (1964) with Gaelic *dealg*, 'thorn', giving 'place of thorns'
DOTHAN	*Dubhachan*, 'black land'
DRUMELDRIE	*Drum*, 'ridge' and *meilearach*, 'sea-grass'
DUNBOG	*Dun*, 'hill fortification', and *bolg*, 'a bag', giving a 'bag-like hill fort'
DUNSHELT	*Dun* and *innis eilt*, 'water-meadow of the cattle'
DYSART	Latin *desertum*, 'desert place', i.e. a hermitage of St Serf
FERNIE	*Fearn*, 'alders', i.e. 'place of alders'
FOODIEASH	*Fodagh*, a grassy place (with ash trees)
FREUCHIE	*Froach*, a heathery place
GLENDUCKIE	*Gleann*, 'glen of the ?'

GLENROTHES	Modern made-up name (1947); *gleann* and title of the Earl of Rothes
GOWKHALL	Scots *gowk*, 'cuckoo' and *hall*, 'bighouse'
HATTON LAW	Scots *hall town*, 'town of the big house' and *law*
INNERLEVEN	'Mouth of the Leven'
INVERKEITHING	Root for mouth and Pictish *Coet*, 'wood/burn'
KEMBACK	*Cearn* and *bac*, 'head of the bend'
KILCONQUHAR	*Cill*, 'church' (of Duncan)
KINCAPLE	*Capull*, 'horse'
KINGHORN	*Gronn*, 'a bog'
KINLOCH	*Ceann da locha*, 'head of two lochs'
LARGO	*Leargach*, 'place on a slope'
LETHAM	*Leatham*, 'broad slope'
LEUCHARS	*Luachair*, 'rushes', i.e. 'place of rushes'
LINDORES	*Lann* and *dorus*, 'chapel at the pass'
LOGIE	*Lug*, 'a hollow'
LUMPHINNANS	*Lann* and *Finan*, 'chapel of St Finan'
METHIL	*Medòn* and *cill*, 'middle church'
MONIMAIL	*Monadh* and *maol*, 'small portion of enclosed land'
PICKLETILLEM	*Pette-talamh*, 'portion of fine land'
RADERNIE	*Rath-airne*, 'fort of the sloe trees'
SALINE	*Sobhal*, 'a barn', i.e. 'place of the barn'
STAR OF MARKINCH	*Stair*, 'path over a bog'
STRATHKINNESS	*Strath*, 'broad valley (of the Kinness Burn)'
TAYPORT	bynamed FERRY-PORT-ON-CRAIG from *port na creige*, 'harbour of the rock'

LOST VILLAGES

Some of Fife's villages have completely vanished. Scattered over Fife, hidden among nettles, brambles and undergrowth, are broken dykes, forming the ruins of towers, houses and cottages that were once a part of a 'lost' hamlet or village, which contributed in their own way to the county's history and heritage.

There is no single reason why these villages all vanished; perhaps they were cleared away by prelate or farmer to establish a new church site or pasture land. Industrial workings, too, caused villages to vanish; depopulation under agriculture or mining decline put paid to others, while more were merged into developing towns.

For those interested in the *earliest* settlements in Fife, the following representative sample presents itself as a basis for further study.

East Lomond Hill and Maiden Castle forts are late first millennium BC to early first millennium AD sites. Norman's Law Fort, four miles north-east of Newburgh, is of similar date and offers summit and terrace relics of dwelling enclosures. Clatchard Craig, Newburgh, the Hut Circles at Hazelton Walls, by Creich, and the Homestead at North Scotstarvit, by Craigrothie are of the same period. Henge monument sites, like the third and second millennium BC examples at Balfarg and Balbirnie, also offer relics of early habitations, as do cairns like that at Saline.

An example of villages which 'vanished' by merger are those of Liberty and Williamsburgh. Once they were separate parts within the burgh barony of Elie, but following the Police Act of 1864 they merged to form a ribbon development of houses along the shore of the Forth from Elie Harbour to Chapel Ness. Bucklyvie's fate, though, offers a more sinister aspect. In 1750 Janet Fall (d.1802) married the eminent judge Sir John Anstruther (d.1811). A society beauty of her day, Janet Fall was the second daughter of Charles Fall, Provost of Dunbar and a descendant of the gypsy Faa's. In those days the village of Bucklyvie stood between the Anstruther property of Elie House and Kilconquhar Loch. According to Janet, the village 'interfered with the privacy of the mansion [of Elie]', and she pressed Sir John to have it removed. Thus the villagers were evicted and the cottar houses raised. This forced disappearance of Bucklyvie inspired Sir Walter Scott to weave the actuality around the eviction of the gypsies from Derncleuch by the Laird of Ellangowan in *Guy Mannering* (1815). Local legend has it that an inhabitant of the doomed Bucklyvie cursed the Anstruthers, as Meg Merrilies cursed Ellangowan, and forecast that only six generations of the family would ever live in the mansion. The prognostication proved true.

The vanished railways of Fife also have a dimension to add to the history of Fife villages. Railway development dated from the days when the Edinburgh and Northern Railway opened its line from Burntisland to Lindores and Cupar in 1847, to the closure of the St Andrews East Fife line to Leven to passenger traffic in 1964.

VILLAGE PROVERBS, SAYINGS AND DOGGEREL

Once the villages – and towns – of Fife inspired a range of proverbs, sayings and doggerel, which became an essential part of the oral fabric of the places. These pieces reflected everyday life, local opinion

and homespun philosophy in a society less literate than today. For
example, here's a proverb popular among handloom weavers:

> Auchtermuchty, Auchtermuchty, payment by piece;
> Cupar o' Fife, Cupar o' Fife, payment by time.

It reflected the change from handloom to power-loom weaving, in
which Auchtermuchty folk were paid by what they produced rather
than by the hours they worked as in Cupar.

One set of village workers might be scathing of the work practices
of others. The folk of Dairsie were wont to decry the agricultural
labourers of Blebo for their dilatoriness with: 'As far behind as the
bandsters [binders of corn] of Blebo'. Whereas the folk of Pathhead
thought themselves shrewder than those of Kirkcaldy; a notion
reflected in the saying: 'You're like Pathhead folk, you look long afore
you'. Villagers often traded insults one habitation with another, like:

> Lundie Mill and Largo, the Kirkton and the Keirs,
> Pittenweem an' Anster are all big leers.*
>
>   *liars

Villagers often expressed their local pride in rhyme; here's one on the
young females of the East Fife fishing villages:

> The lasses o' the Ferry[1]
> They busk braw;[2]
> The lasses o'the Elie.
> They ding a';[3]
> The lasses o'St Monan,
> They curse and ban;[4]
> The lasses o'Pittenweem,
> They do the same;
> The lasses o'Anster,
> They drink strong ale;
> There's green grass in Cellardyke,
> And crabs in till Crail.
>
>   [1] Earlsferry
>   [2] dress well
>   [3] beat all for looks
>   [4] swear

Children were often taught by local doggerel. Here's how fisher
children from North Queensferry learned to plot the water route
from their village to the Tay:

Inchcolm, Inchkeith, the twa Mickeries and Craigleith,
The lofty Bass and the Isle of May, round the Car and in the Tay.

Finally, too, the weather was reflected in village rhyme, perhaps forming the greatest amount of local folk matter: here's what the old folk of the East Neuk said about sowing and reaping in their areas:

Lathoddie, Radernie, Lathockar, and Lathones
Ye may saw wi'gloves aff, and shear wi'mittens on.

THE FIFE VILLAGE YEAR

As elsewhere in Scotland, the pattern of Fife village life was always geared to the perennial cycle of ploughing, sowing and reaping; new crops and first fruits. The weeks of hard work required by agriculture and animal husbandry were counterbalanced with periods of relaxation, with their traditional fairs, festivals and holidays, and these in turn forged a colourful folk year in Fife largely suppressed by the sixteenth-century reformers.

The early settlers in Fife followed what might be called the seasonal festivals of the Celtic peoples, listed below.

> 1 February: Oimelc, or Imbolc. Corresponding to the Christian
> Candlemas or St Bride's Day
> 1 May: Bealltan – May Day
> 1 August: Lugnassad – Lammas
> 1 November: Samhuinn – Hallowe'en

In the Celtic calendar these were important religious and judicial days that were later associated with festivals and sports, although their original intent was the growing and reaping of crops and the movement of cattle to and from summer and winter pasture. These too were important days of *saining*, the ritual blessing of animals and property, along with divination of future tribal group prosperity.

As the Christian missionaries spread the Gospel in the areas now known as Scotland the old tribal festive days were given Christian overtones and there developed the Scots Quarter Days:

> 2 February: Candlemas
> 15 May: Whitsun, or Old Beltane
> 1 August: Lammas
> 11 November: Martinmas, or Old Hallowmas

On these days Fife agricultural workers were hired at special 'hiring fairs', wages were paid and rents and feus were rendered. But the Fife village year was more complicated than just the Quarter Day rituals:

1 January: Ne'er Day (New Year's Day)

The ancient Celtic New Year began with the entry of winter on 1 November.

Up to 1599 Fife folk marked New Year's Day as 25 March: this was changed by James VI's Act of the Privy Council (December 1599) ordaining 1 January as New Year's Day. In Fife it was a day of family gatherings, and such public displays as processions by Freemasons; the latter were a relic of the medieval processions by the Trades Guilds.

Auld Handsel Monday (the first Monday after 1 January)

Up to the end of the nineteenth century this was the day when Fife farm labourers, domestic servants and industrial workers had a day's holiday. This was usually accompanied by a *handsel* (good luck gift) of money, clothes, or food. Sometimes a laird would fund a communal meal for his estate workers. It was also a day for family visits, and a parish social or two.

Lord Shaw of Dunfermline remembered how Auld Hansel Monday was a prime holiday in the town:

> At Dunfermline the one day stretched into three. Still the traffic in merchandise, in sweets by the hundredweight and gingerbread by the load ... [Fife] emptied itself into the town, and even the sedate residents slipped from their houses to the booths, the children breaking from their parents' guard and getting hilariously lost. For these last there were presents, a chance upon chance – sweets from Kirkcaldy, fruit from the Carse of Gowrie –and in their uncivilised minds it was a glorious holiday.

This festive day was the relic of Uphalieday.

6 January: Uphalieday

Uphalieday, or Twelfth Night, is the Christian feast of Epiphany. In medieval Scotland this was a great court festival interlarded with guisards (mummers), pageantries and plays, led by a mock director of revels in 'The King of the Bean'. In particular there might be an enactment of *Ane Satyre of the Thrie Estates*, by the Monimail-born Sir David Lindsay of the Mount (*c.*1486–1555), which was first performed at Castlehill, Cupar. Court Uphalieday revels were known in Fife when the court was in residence at Falkland Palace. Some Fife village folk prepared and ate a Twelfth Night cake upon this day.

25 January: Burns Night (the celebration of the birth of Robert Burns in 1759)

Although the first Burns Club was founded around 1801 at Green-ock, Burns Suppers have always been popular in Fife's villages, particularly in the mining and working-class areas where Burns has been identified as a socialist icon. The Bowhill's People's Burns Club, first established by members of the Communist Party in 1925, is one of the most active of the eleven Burns Clubs in Fife.

1–2 February: Candlemas

The old Celtic feast of spring was celebrated in the Fife medieval Church as the Feast of St Bride. Clerics grafted the celebration of St Bride of Kildare (452–525) on to the day dedicated to a Celtic goddess of a similar name. Candlemas Eve (1 February) became the Eve of the Purification of the Blessed Virgin.

In Fife's superstitious lore it was the eve when witches met in coven.

14 February: St Valentine's Day

The day in which lovers exchanged Valentines, and Fife folk indul-ged in divination to discover the names of future spouses.

Fastern's E'en

A moveable feast, the equivalent of Shrove Tuesday.

A popular time for cockfights in Fife, whose patron was James VI, although historians aver that the 'sport' was introduced to Scotland by Prince James, Duke of York (later King James VII and II) who was Lord High Commissioner to the Parliament of Scotland in 1681, and who resided for a while at Elie.

Up to the Second World War Lochgelly still offered cockfighting as a diversion, although it had been illegal since 1849.

Pasch: the moveable Feast of Easter

Medieval Fife folk ate a dish of roasted peas on Car Sunday, the fifth Sunday of Lent. Although the reformers frowned on all such 'popish' relics of Easter ceremonial, the baking of Easter hot-cross buns and the decoration of Easter eggs was once very popular in Fife's villages.

1 April: Gowkin' Day

This was Fife's Festival of Fools, an event probably introduced to the county (and Scotland) by French courtiers importing their mummery of *Poissons d'Avril*. A 'gowk', from the Scots word for cuckoo, was sent on fools' errands.

Links Market, Kirkcaldy (mid-April)
The still surviving market is said to have originated as an Easter Fair in 1305.

1 May: Beltane
The Celtic fire festival in honour of the sun, when the tribesfolk of Fife went forth to hunt and fish, mimicking their mythical chieftain figure Fingal, leader of the Fianna hunters.

A bonfire lit on this day, to burn through to 2 May, was deemed to guarantee the cleansing of an area of witchcraft and evil spirits. For the same reason rowan branches were collected, some to be made into *roks* (spinning wheels) and spindles, a May dew was collected in which to bathe faces to enhance beauty.

Midsummer Eve
Midsummer Festival Games at Ceres. On this festival folklorist Florence Marian McNeill (1885–1973) had this to say: 'The village festival appears to be unique in Scotland, for it is believed to have been established in 1314 by the men of Ceres on their triumphal return from the Battle of Bannockburn, and has been held every year since.' The games are held on the green known as the Bow Butts; the latter name appears in various village locations in Fife to indicate where archery practice took place in medieval times.

29 June
On this day the medieval East Neuk fishermen celebrated the feast day of St Peter the Apostle, the Galilean fisherman who was called with his elder brother Andrew, patron saint of Scotland, to be disciples of Christ.

July
The month in which the Whipmen – carters and chapmen – held their celebrations and races. Here is what one anonymous hand recorded of the annual Chapman's Tournament at Leslie, at 'Christ's Kirk on the Green':

> The pedlars, or packmen, by tilting at a ring, endeavoured to imitate the chivalrous knights of old. Much merriment was excited whenever these

doughty pedlars – their horses at full strength – missed striking the ring…
as it inevitably followed that the circumstance caused them to drop both
reins and spear and cling convulsively to the saddle…

At this time of year the folk of Newburgh undertook the 'Walking of
the Marches'. From the East Port the villagers, preceded by the town
band and civic dignitaries, processed over the spurs of the Ochils and
monitored the March Stones which long set out the limits of their
boundaries.

To mark their summer festivities the folk of Newburgh also held a
Salmon-Cobble Race. There was a street fair, too, moved to this date
from Martinmas, as the old village doggerel remembered:

> It fell about the Martinmas time,
> And a gay time it was then, O,
> When our gudwife had puddens to mak'
> And she boiled them in a pan, O.

1 July: St Serf's Festival at Culross
Provision and market up to Reformation.

1 August: Lammas
The Celtic festival of autumn. A season of fairs, an important one
being at St Andrews.

A Sea Harvest Thanksgiving was held at St Monans.

29 September: Michaelmas
The Feast Day of Michael the Victorious, patron of Fife's seashores,
boats, boatmen, horses and horsemen.

31 October: Hallowe'en
The Celtic feast of Samhuinn, the entry of winter, and the rituals of
the cult of the dead. Around encampments skulls of the dead were
placed on poles, from which Fife folk obtained their custom of making
turnip lanterns with grotesque faces. Grafted on to this was the
Christian Feast of All Saints, the liturgical honouring of the Blessed
Dead – in Fife folklore the time of fairy flittings, witch activity and
divining the future.

11 November: Martinmas, or Old Hallowe'en
The Feast of St Martin of Tours, a popular saint in Fife.

30 November: Anermas, St Andrew's Day

An important festival for Fife folk, proud owners of the relics of St Andrew the Apostle in St Andrews Cathedral. As Sir David Lindsay pointed out, the St Andrew's Day dinner was an important court function: at Falkland James IV offered his guests 'wilde fowle, venisoun and wyne, with tairt and flam and fruitage fyne'. The day when Fife folk hunted rabbits and squirrels.

25 December–6 January (Twelfth Night): the Feast of Yule

The Scandinavian Feast of *Iol*, or Yule, Christianised as Christmas. Following the abolition of papal authority and the Scottish Parliament's ratification of the Protestant faith in June and August 1560, Christmas was banned in Scotland. In 1574 one William Bell, a baker of St Andrews, was reported to the religious authorities for baking the traditional Yule loaf and offering it to guests at his house; his fate is unknown. But in medieval Fife the Twelve Days of Christmas, the Daft Days, were celebrated with a will. During the military occupation of Scotland in Cromwellian times up to 1660 any Christmas revelry was severely stamped out.

26 December: Holy Innocents' Day

A special medieval festival for Fife's choirboys and scholars from church schools, particularly celebrated at Dunfermline, Cupar and St Andrews.

VILLAGE VISITORS

Because of its situation and focal points of national importance, from meeting places for parliaments like Dairsie Castle and St Andrews Cathedral to royal palaces like Dunfermline and Falkland, Fife villages received a range of visitors who were able to observe and comment on their characters.

One such visitor was the novelist and journalist Daniel Defoe (1660–1731). An extremely versatile and prolific writer, Defoe's career was somewhat in the doldrums until he was rescued by Robert Harley, 1st Earl of Oxford (1661–1724), the Tory statesman and bibliophile, who employed him as a secret agent between 1703–14. Thus Defoe travelled round the country for Harley – and also Sydney, 1st Earl Godolphin – to observe the mood of the nation and test the political temperature. Such a secret mission brought him to Fife.

Although Defoe's best-known work was to be *Robinson Crusoe* (1719), with Largo-born Alexander Selkirk as its hero inspiration, Defoe left some notes on the places in Fife that he visited. Defoe crossed the Forth from South Queensferry and entered Fife, which he dubbed 'Old Caledonia', at Inverkeithing. Of it he commented: '[a] walled town still populous though greatly decayed'; at Dunfermline he noted 'the full perfection of decay', but he went on, 'the people would be poorer if they had not the manufacture of linen – the damask and better sort being carried on here'.

Defoe visited the Earl of Morton's castle of Aberdour and Falkland Palace, remarking that the Scottish kings had had more royal palaces than their English counterparts. At Leslie he visited the seat of the Earl of Rothes and declared it 'the glory of the place and the whole province of Fife'. He admired the work that Oliver Cromwell's masons had done at Burntisland harbour and how the little coastal villages of Fife produced the 'green cloth, which is in great demand in England for the printing trade, in the room of calicoes, which have been for some years prohibited'. Kinghorn folk he found were being supported by the thread trade which the women manufactured when their menfolk were at sea, and he marvelled at the 'considerable corn merchants' of Kirkcaldy and the 'salt-work and a few nailers' of Dysart. Strange to tell, Defoe makes no comment on the collieries of Fife, although he did visit Culross and must have been aware of the coalmines sponsored by the Bruces. At Leven he noted that the villagers 'bred the best salmon in Scotland' and noted in particular the 'good harbours' of the coastal villages.

Defoe's reports were to be of great use to his political masters and his comments on the potential for commerce in such places as Fife were part of the propaganda which led to the securing of agreement for the Treaty of Union of 1707. In his Fife report Defoe noted that the decline he saw was a consequence of the 'ecclesiastical capital' of Scotland (meaning St Andrews) becoming redundant at the Reformation and the shift of the royal court to Greenwich in 1603. He also saw Fife gentry as laggards in their county's promotion; he believed that 'like true patriots' they should have sustained their own settlements.

Another visitor to Fife's villages, when the county was a web of such settlements, was the pioneer traveller and tourist Richard Pococke (1704–65). In the late 1730s and early 1740s Pococke had explored Asia Minor and Greece and pioneered alpine travel. By the time that he came to Fife, in August 1760, he was Episcopal Bishop of Ossory in the Province of Dublin. Although Pococke was particularly concerned with ecclesiastical antiquities of the county, his comments on other Fife matters are worthy of note.

On 29 August 1760 Pococke crossed the Tay at Newburgh and noted how 'even the poorest classes' in the village were keen on self-education, and how the Seceders' movement – the departure from the Church of Scotland in 1732 of certain ministers to form the Secession Church – promoted education in 'frugal colleges' for all. While in the area Pococke visited the sandstone boulder with eight cupmarks atop known as Macduff's Cross. Here he heard the village tales of how the cross was the rallying-sanctuary point for the clan Macduff, the patronymic of the Celtic earls of Fife. Pococke was further intrigued by the village witch superstitions. In 1610 Grissell Gairdner of Newburgh was executed (at Edinburgh) for practising 'sorcerie' in the village; in 1653 Katherine Kay of Newburgh was exposed as one of a family of supposed witches; and there were other witchcraft cases in 1661 and 1662.

From Newburgh, via Cupar and St Andrews, Pococke visited the East Neuk villages. In his subsequent volume *Tour Through Scotland* he had this to say of his visit to Elie, with a comment on a Fife laird:

Another mile brought us to Elly [Pococke's spellings have not been altered], where there is a harbour for large Ships, and on the east side of it is a rock of freestone in which they find Garnites; and being set with a foil, they look like rubies and are so called. From this place I went to Elly House, close to it, and visited Sir John Anstruther. It is a good house built to an old castle, there are some good pictures in it, particularly Copies of some of the Luxemburgh Gallery. Sir John has a good Collection of books, also of the Roman Coins, with some Greek, and several Modern Medals collected by his father, who laid out this place in very good taste, and made Plantations on each side of the lawn before the house; and there are four terraces round the woods; In the front is the Firth of Forth, and to the west the bay of Largo appears like a great river.

Balgonie, Kellie and Lundin castles fell under the bishop's eye as did the three large standing stones at Lundin Links which he opined were 'doubtless an Antient Druid temple'. After viewing the colliery settlements around Leven he visited the Earl of Rothes at Leslie House, a particular interest to him as Rothes was then commander-in-chief of the British army in Ireland. After brief visits to Falkland and Kirkcaldy the bishop left the county via Culross. 'Robust and characterful' was how he described the villagers of Fife.

In 1773 the Scots lawyer and writer James Boswell (1740–95) persuaded his friend Dr Samuel Johnson (1709–84) to visit Scotland. So, almost twenty years before Boswell was to become world famous with his biography of the distinguished lexicographer, he and Johnson entered Fife. Boswell was to keep a detailed note of what they encountered, published later in *Journal of a Tour of the Hebrides* (1785).

On Wednesday 18 August 1773, Boswell, Johnson and their respective servants, the negro Francis Barber and the 'Bohemian' Joseph Ritter, set out from Edinburgh to Fife, accompanied by lawyer William Nairne – later Lord Dunsinane – who was of the party as far as St Andrews. Boswell averred that the prospect over the Firth of Forth, looking towards Fife, was 'the finest in Europe', and won the reply from Johnson: 'Water is the same everywhere'. Johnson further remarked at the number of barefoot folk he saw as they travelled. As they crossed the Forth Johnson asked that the ferryman pause at Inchkeith Island; this he said would be a fine place for a mansion with garden and vines, a good investment if properly developed, but nearer to London.

The party landed at Kinghorn and dined at Munro's on fish with onion sauce, roast mutton and potatoes. Then boarding a post-chaise they cut across Fife to Cupar 'and drank tea'. Boswell remarked that they 'had a dreary drive in a dusky night to St Andrews' where they put up at Glass's Inn to dine on 'rissered haddocks and mutton chops'.

The famous literary pair stayed at St Andrews for two nights, while Johnson viewed the university, met some of its academics and assessed the cathedral ruins. By this time St Andrews was in some decay. Some ten years later, Francis Douglas of Abbots Inch wrote:

> It is truly humiliating to see a noble street [South Street] almost without inhabitants terminated by the august ruins of a church so long the boast of this city. It is supposed that not above an eighth part of it is now inhabited. It appears from the account received that there were at some times 153 brewers in it; there are but 30 at present. There were 53 bakers; now there are only four.

One St Andrews resident to whom Johnson was introduced was Colonel Nairne, who invited him to view his garden and grotto. Here Johnson was shown 'a fine old plane tree'. Nairne boasted that there was only one other large tree like it in Fife. This amused Johnson who remarked that he had seen few substantial trees as he had ridden through the villages of Fife.

On 20 August Boswell and Johnson left St Andrews for Dundee, pausing at Leuchars. Boswell noted:

> The manse, as the parsonage-house is called in Scotland, was close by [the church]. I waited on the minister, mentioned our names, and begged he would tell us what he knew about it. He was a very civil old man, but could only inform us that it was supposed to have stood eight hundred years. He told us there was a colony of Danes in his parish; that they had landed at a remote period of time, and still remained a distinct people. Dr Johnson shrewdly inquired whether they had brought women with them.

The notion that Leuchars villagers were descendants of Vikings was later scorned by Sir Walter Scott as 'vain imagination'.

'I never saw so many good houses of people of family and fortune as in this part of Fife'. So wrote Sir Walter Scott of the East Neuk. He visited the area during the weekend of 13–16 June 1823, with Sir Henry Raeburn and the Blair Adam Club. Scott knew Fife reasonably well: he had first visited St Andrews in 1793 and his son married a Jobson of Lochore House. Several of his books, such as *The Heart of Midlothian* (1818), contain hints of East Neuk history and legend and his *Guy Mannering* (1815) has an inspirational theme of a vanished village near Elie House.

Another writer was to add to the contemporary assessment of Fife folk and their settlements. The essayist and historian Thomas Carlyle (1795–1881) was born at Ecclefechan, Dumfriesshire, the son of a stonemason. Although intended for the church, Carlyle studied mathematics at Edinburgh University and in 1816 took up a teaching post as schoolmaster at the Burgh School, Kirkcaldy, at £80 per annum. Carlyle was able to observe how the small towns and villages of Fife were starting to revive after their gradual decline following the Reformation. Alone, or with such as his friend Edward Irving, he explored the villages of south Fife, with excursions to the Lomonds to watch surveyors preparing new maps of the county. His writing too, began to reflect what he thought of Fife folk. At Kirkcaldy he found 'a pleasant, honest kind of fellow-mortals, something of quietly fruitful, of good old Scotch in their works and ways, more vernacular, peaceable, fixed, and almost genial in their mode of life, than I had been used to in the Border'.

Of Fife folk in general he said: 'I always rather liked the people' and he admired their fortitude against often unfavourable circumstances in 'the little burghs and sea villages, with their poor little havens, salt-panns, and weather-beaten bits of cyclopean breakwaters, and rude innocent machineries ... looms, Baltic trade, and whale-fishing, and the flax-mills turned mainly by wind and curious blue-painted wheels with oblique vans.' Carlyle remained in Kirkcaldy long enough to see the first steamer to appear on the Forth around 1818. This with the subsequent railway developments opened up the county to a wider range of visitors with more experiences to gather and opinions to express.

GAZETTEER

ABERCROMBIE

At one time the name of the area in and around the village of St Monans was known as Abercrombie, and it appears in records as a parish as early as 1174. In 1646 the barony of St Monans was added and the whole was called St Monans until in 1804 the name Abercrombie was reinstated. The land on which modern Abercrombie stands was owned in the eleventh century by John Cocus, said to have been cook to the royal household of Malcolm III. Local tradition has it that a chapel was founded here around 1160 by Mary Cocus and Margaret, Lady de Candelle, daughters of John Cocus, and consecrated to St Monan and the Blessed Virgin by Arnold, Bishop of St Andrews; the building was rededicated by Bishop David de Bernham of St Andrews in 1247. Around 1315 Humphry de Abercrombie received a charter of title from Robert the Bruce (r. 1306–39), and his family founded the genealogical house of Abercrombie. Regarding Abercrombie chapel's history we are on surer ground with the record that William I, the Lion (r.1165–1214), granted the chapel to the abbey of Dunfermline and his grant was confirmed by Alexander II (r. 1214–49) and Alexander III (r. 1249–86). In 1421, by the Bulls of Pope Martin V, the chapel was given to the Augustinian priory of St Andrews. The shell of the late-medieval chapel was used as a burial ground for the Abercrombies of that Ilk, who sold the estate in 1646, and later the Anstruthers of Balcaskie.

The family of Abercrombie of that Ilk supplied the last medieval abbot of Inchcolm in Richard Abercrombie, who in 1543 resigned his abbey in favour of James Stewart, Lord Doune, as Commendator. Abercrombie continued to head the religious community until his death on 26 March 1549. The village name also appeared in the title of the Sandilands family, the Lords Abercrombie, who by 1647 owned nearby Newark Castle.

Today the village of white harled cottages sits off the B942. Tradition has it that Abercrombie Farm (1892) lies on the site of the mansion built by John Cocus' son Richard in 1260. Abercrombie's important architectural neighbour is Balcaskie House.

Balcaskie House

When the monarchy was restored with the return of Charles II to Whitehall on his thirtieth birthday in 1660, the Scottish nobility received a boost with the restoration of the Scottish Parliament, the Privy Council and the Law Courts. Cromwell's military occupation of Scotland had thwarted the Fife nobility who were determined to assert their refound influence. To this end they set about a new phase of building. Thus Balcaskie House became an early Restoration project in Fife for the new laird Sir William Bruce (*c.* 1630–1710), who during 1668–74 enlarged the extant laird's tower-house (*c.* 1629) which had been in the ownership of the Moncrieffs. The terraced gardens were also laid out by Bruce to have a focal point towards the Bass Rock in the Forth; the frontal garden was the first substantial Italian garden in Scotland. During 1684 Bruce sold the property to Sir Thomas Steuart and in 1698 it was acquired by Sir Robert Anstruther, whose later family made alterations to the fabric of the buildings. The lodges are of early Victorian date and the Home Farm of 1834–35. Mid-eighteenth century doocots are still extant.

ABERDOUR

Modern Aberdour, bifurcated by the Dour burn, is made up of two medieval village sites within the 1640 parish of the same name. Easter Aberdour was made a burgh of regality in 1383, and Wester Aberdour was a burgh of barony from 1501. Easter Aberdour owed its title to the Douglas family, the earls of Morton, while Wester Aberdour was a barony under the Abbey of St Colme on Inchcolm and the Stewart earls of Moray.

Once known for its weaving, coal and freestone quarries, with a mention of corn mills in early medieval times, Wester Aberdour developed in the nineteenth century as a seaside resort for the middle classes, while its Easter neighbour was dominated by the railway station, a key link in past days making Aberdour the 'Fife Riviera'. Today the location retains some fine eighteenth- and nineteenth-century buildings.

Aberdour was noted in medieval times for its Hospital of St Martha, founded in 1474 by James, Earl of Morton, assisted by his Countess Anne. It was intended for the maintenance of the poor and to provide hospitality for pilgrims and wayfarers under the care of the Sisters of Penitence of the Third Order of St Francis. The old church of St Fillan's, standing by the road leading to the Silver Sands beach, is a Scottish ecclesiastical gem. Once the church was part of the endowments of the Abbey of Inchcolm (*c.*1128), and its nave and chancel are of around 1140. It sports additions of 1500 and 1608, but was unroofed at the completion of a new parish church in the High Street of 1787–90. St Fillan's was restored 1925–6. Local legend has it that Robert the Bruce, thought to be a leper, worshipped at the now sealed leper's squint at St Fillan's after the Battle of Bannockburn in 1314.

The half-ruined Aberdour Castle has had a history from around the thirteenth century when a castle here formed the capital messuage of the barony of Aberdour, granted by Robert I, The Bruce, to his nephew Thomas Randolph, Earl of Moray, in 1325. In 1342 Sir William Douglas of Liddesdale acquired a charter of the barony from the Morays and the property has remained in the Douglas family ever since. The oldest part of the castle is the fourteenth-century rhomboidal tower, now a part of the west range with other buildings added during the sixteenth and seventeenth centuries. The construction of the garden terraces to the south in the seventeenth century and the sculpting of the nineteenth-century railway embankment to the north altered the early medieval character of the site. In history Aberdour Castle is remembered as a principal home of James Douglas, 4th Earl of Morton, Regent of Scotland from 1572 until the *coup d'état* of 1578. Before his execution in 1581 Morton is said to have 'denuded the royal treasury' and hidden his booty at Aberdour.

Aberdour harbour in the 1890s. An important haven from before the days of Charles I, in whose reign it became a burgh of barony. The village was supported by agriculture, manufactures and handicrafts. [*Staralp*]

Shore Street leads down to the late eighteenth-century harbour built by the then Earl of Morton for the shipment of limestone from his quarries; before the coming of the railway a pinnace sailed twice a week for Leith. Two-storeyed Aberdour House, at the north end of the High Street, was a townhouse of the Mortons and dates from the seventeenth and eighteenth centuries.

ANSTRUTHER

Historically Anstruther is made up of two component parts, Anstruther Easter and Anstruther Wester. Until 1641 Anstruther Easter was in the parish of Kilrenny and was recorded as the smallest parish in Scotland.

Anstruther Easter

In the reign of David I (1124–53) the lands of Anstruther Easter were held by the Anglo-Norman William de Candelle, Lord of Anstruther. By the reign of Malcolm IV (1153–65), William de Candelle's son gave *tres bothas* (three shops) in the village to the Premonstratensian

Early Victorian Anstruther from the south-west looking across to the harbour where the Dreel Burn marks the ancient boundary between Easter and Wester Anstruther. The sixteenth-century bell tower of St Adrian's Church Hall (formerly the parish church) lies to the left. [*Author's collection*]

monks of Dryburgh Abbey, Berwickshire. Thereafter the direct descendants of the de Candelles, the Anstruthers, became superiors of the area until modern times. At that time the Anstruthers inhabited the Castle of Dreel. Many of the Anstruthers acquired important court prerogatives; for instance, Sir James Anstruther was appointed Hereditary Carver to James VI in 1585. Anstruther Easter became a burgh of barony in 1572 and a royal burgh in 1585, ratified in 1587. The Castle of Dreel, set by the Dreel Burn (with stone fragments still seen in walls at Wightman's Wynd), had vanished by the 1800s although it was reasonably habitable in 1732. Still a stronghold in 1651, the castle was used as a deposit by the burghers for their 'most precious goods' when Cromwell's army descended on the burgh; alas the goods were lost when the castle fell to the Ironsides. Here King Charles II was entertained by Sir Philip Anstruther after his coronation in January 1651.

As well as the Castle of Dreel, settlement expansion areas in Anstruther Easter included the land around St Adrian's Church, built by public subscription in 1634; a spire was erected around 1644 and the whole was repaired in 1834. A manse was established here at Backdykes in 1590.

Anstruther Easter forms the central core of modern Anstruther with a prominent focal point at Shore Street and the harbour, exhibiting a range of seventeenth- and eighteenth-century buildings. The mercat cross of 1677 is sited in Shore Street. Once known for its shipbuilding and fish processing, the port of Anstruther was officially established with a customs house in 1710. The central pier probably dates from the sixteenth century, with a West Pier of 1753, and an East Pier formed 1866–77. Before 1914 Anstruther was deemed the capital of the winter herring fishing industry. The Scottish Fisheries Museum takes pride of place at Harbourhead on a site once owned by the Abbey of Balmerino, and here a fine overview of the history of Anstruther can be found.

The dividing line between Easter and Wester Anstruther is the Dreel Burn, the Dreel Bridge (1630), rebuilt 1795, resited 1831, leading the High Street into the western development.

Anstruther Wester

Once conferred on the priory of Pittenweem, this location was erected into a burgh of barony in 1540, confirmed in 1554, and was created a royal burgh by James VI in 1587 and confirmed in 1592. Like its Easter counterpart Anstruther Wester was a habitation for fishermen and sailors, much affected commercially by the 1707 Act of Union, when the trade in malt, herring and cod declined. Prior to this too, the settlements suffered much in the Civil Wars when Anstruther Covenanters fell at the battle of Kilsyth (1645).

As the High Street sweeps west into Pittenweem Road (A917), the area is dominated by the late eighteenth-century Town Hall abutting St Adrian's Church Hall (the original parish church) and the *c.* sixteenth-century steeple, once a part of the eighteenth-century revamped medieval church. The whole overlooks the estuary of the Dreel Burn with relics of a seventeenth-century harbour, ruined by the early 1700s. In this area too are some interesting seventeenth- and eighteenth-century buildings including the Dreel Tavern in High Street, a former coach inn. The late sixteenth-century Smuggler's Inn in High Street recalls the days when this area by the Dreel Burn was the haunt of smugglers. Records show that the Anstruthers were affected by piracy in past ages for the burghers often applied to the government to be excused levies as they had suffered deprivation from piracy.

One of the most curious Anstruther associations was The Most Ancient and Puissant Order of the Beggar's Benison and Merryland, founded in 1732 as a gentleman's club devoted to libidinous interests. It met twice a year at Candlemas and St Andrew's Day at the old Castle of Dreel in a chamber called the Temple, and later at Anstruther hostelries. The membership was made up of notable local worthies from the Earl of Kellie to local ministers, doctors, merchants and shipmasters. The club is thought to have terminated in 1836.

Anstruther has had a range of 'local village heroes'. Few would leave out William Tennant (1784–1848) in such a list. Although he trained for the ministry and later occupied the Chair of Oriental Languages at St Mary's College, St Andrews, Tennant is famed for his verses – *Anster Fair* was one of the most popular comic poems ever produced in the early nineteenth century. Some aver its Italian *ottava rima* stanza form even inspired Lord Byron.

One 'hero' added a romantic tale that persists. Along School Green is Melville's Manse, built in 1590 and restored in 1977. It was constructed for James Melville (1556–1614), whose *Autobiography and Diary* is a valuable account of his ministry at Anstruther; Melville was the nephew of the famous founder of Scottish presbyterianism, Andrew Melville (1545–1622). The story is still remembered of how Melville acted as a negotiator when survivors of the Spanish Armada supply ship *El Gran Grifton* arrived at Anstruther on 6 December 1588. One of the Spanish grandees, General Don Juan Gomez de Medina, came ashore with his retinue and explained what had befallen the Spanish fleet; de Medina had himself been wrecked on Fair Isle and made passage in a hired ship to Anstruther. The Anstruther folk gave sincere hospitality to the Spaniards, the local story goes, which was repaid in a fortuitous way. On his way home de Medina called in at Cadiz, where he found a shipwrecked Anstruther fishing crew impounded by the authorities. The Commander pleaded the case of the Anstruther fishermen to the Spanish king and obtained their release.

ARNCROACH

Formerly known as Aldenroch, the village of Arncroach lies to the west of Kellie Castle in the lee of Kellie Law, and originated in the eighteenth century as an agricultural hamlet within the parish of Carnbee. Historically dominated by the barony of Kellie, the land came to the Oliphants, via a messuage of the Siwards, in 1361.

Turreted and crowstepped Kellie Castle represents a fine sixteenth- and seventeenth-century Scots mansion with a probable fifteenth-century tower. Financial difficulties caused the Oliphants to sell the property to Thomas Erskine, Viscount Fenton and later Earl of Kellie, in 1617; his descendants held it until the then abandoned castle was leased by Professor James Alan Lorimer who rescued the property, although Lorimer's son Sir Robert Stodart Lorimer (1864–1929) was the prime mover in the restoration of the castle. The walled garden was laid out in 1880. The whole was purchased by the National Trust for Scotland in 1970.

Associated with Arncroach, Carnbee Free Church dates from 1844–5, while neighbouring Gibliston House (bought by Sir Robert Lorimer in 1916 for his own use) is an early nineteenth-century villa. The hand of Sir Robert is also seen in Lundie Cottage, Arncroach, which he enlarged in 1903 for his blacksmith.

AUCHMUTY AND BALBIRNIE MILLS

Auchmuty was once the seat of the family known as Auchmuty of that Ilk. Their property was centred on the farm of Auchmuty and the family were prominent Fife medieval gentry; one David de Admuty (sic) was among the 8,000 Scots slain at Flodden in 1513. During his levée at Wemyss Castle in 1651, Charles II knighted another David Auchmuty, but the family fell on hard times – through profligacy, legend has it. The property was then acquired by John, Earl of Rothes, in 1670. Ten years later, on 29 May 1680, Charles II elevated the earl to Duke of Rothes and his gazetted titles included Lord Auchmoutye (sic). Today Auchmuty's original hamlet of estate houses is absorbed into Glenrothes new town.

Old gazetteers used to combine the houses associated with the woollen and barley mills of Balbirnie Mills, across the River Leven, with Auchmuty, but the area is dominated today by the mother parish of Markinch and the paper mill by the river.

Around Balbirnie

Balbirnie Bridge: *c.*1792; replaced bridge of 1710 on the ancient cross-Fife route.

Balbirnie Estate: first mentioned as property of John de Balbrenny (sic) in 1312; held by that family until the fifteenth century. Estate divided *c.*1540 into various ownerships.

Balbirnie House: mansion built 1815 for General Robert Balfour on the site of a seventeenth-century house given a new front block in

Balbirnie House

1772–82; park and walled garden, 1779–86; now a country house hotel.

AUCHTERDERRAN

Although a portion of its acres were once a part of Ballingry parish, and known as Kirkindorath, from 1890 the enlarged Auchterderran retained its ancient status and hamlet with Loch Gelly at its south-western boundary. Today it is almost swamped by the old mining communities of Bowhill and Cardenden. Once known in Fife for its cattle, butter, cheese and poultry, Auchterderran owed its prosperity to coalmining with seven flourishing pits at the turn of the twentieth century. Records suggest that the church of Auchterderran was a dependency on the monastery of St Serf, Kinross, given as a gift by the Celtic Bishop Fothad (fl.s 1059–93); an unauthenticated source also suggests the medieval hospital of Innerlochty was sited hereabouts. The church was rededicated by David de Bernham, Bishop of St Andrews in 1244. Of this original church few traces are extant, and the existing T-plan church dates from 1789 with enlargements and alterations. Relics of the previous church graveyard exist; one such is the piend-roofed burial aisle of the Kininmonths of that Ilk. Within the old parish stood the tower of Carden. The estate of Carden was the heritage of the Mertynes, but fell to the Crown. In

1582 James VI gifted it to George Martene with its mineral rights, mills and woods; thereafter it passed to the Wemyss family and the earls of Leven. The medieval devotion to the Celtic Fothad is remembered in St Fothad's Parish Church, Carden Avenue, built 1909–10. Writing in 1790 the parish minister the Rev. Andrew Murray noted that the agricultural day labourer at Auchterderran had a weekly pay rate of six shillings (30p), compared with the collier at ten shillings (50p).

AUCHTERMUCHTY

In Fife's early history the lands that make up the parish of Auchtermuchty were in the hands of the earls of Fife. In time they were disponed to Robert, Duke of Albany, but were merged with the Crown on the fall of Murdoch, Duke of Albany, in 1425. Up to the sixteenth century Auchtermuchty was divided into the North Quarter and the South Quarter, which developed on the rising ground overlooking the Howe of Fife. In 1517 James V elevated the lands of Auchtermuchty into a royal burgh, with the usual privileges including the right to hold a market on Wednesdays and an annual eight-day fair on the Feast of St Serf (2 June). From this time Auchtermuchty began to expand, with a development of wooden, stone and thatched houses (the rushes coming from Lindores Loch), and throughout the sixteenth century properties were associated with many important personages at court from George Setoun, adherent of Mary, Queen of Scots and John Paterson, Carrick Herald. Mary Livingstone – one of the 'Four Maries' – was given land at Auchtermuchty as a wedding present when she married John Sempill of Beltrees. James VI renewed the burgh's privileges in 1591, as did Charles I in 1631.

Once a place of linen handlooms (the last fell silent in 1912), with a flour, corn and lint mill and iron foundry, Auchtermuchty still reflects a core village which developed as a minor nineteenth-century industrial centre. Auchtermuchty had a parish church dedicated to St Mary and St Andrew in medieval times, a gift in 1350 of Duncan, Earl of Fife, to the Abbey of Lindores. The extant church was erected 1779–81 but has later additions. In the 1790s the minister was still paid a stipend in measures of barley and oats as well as money; a manse was completed in 1792. Auchtermuchty often had colourful parish ministers: James Bennet held the parish from 1615–40 and was 'gravelie rebuikit' as a 'frequent hunter with dogs, ane player at

Auchtermuchty looking across the Howe of Fife. The spire of the parish church, 1779–81, and the Town Hall tower, 1728, dominate the village skyline. [*Author's collection*]

cards, and a runner of horses upon courses'.

Auchtermuchty Townhouse of 1728 stands in the High Street across from where the old mercat cross was sited, a place now marked by the war memorial of 1919–20. Another neighbour is Macduff House (1597) with its eighteenth-century interior panelling and original staircases.

Within the parish is Myres Castle, once a property of the earls of Fife. By 1454 the estate was in the hands of John Scrymgeour, Macer and Sergeant at Arms to the king, whose descendants secured tenure as important courtiers. In 1634 the property was bought by the Covenanting General John Leslie. It remains as a basic sixteenth-century laird's house developed as a nineteenth-century mansion with a walled garden of 1890.

Another property worth noting is Rossie House, which dates from around 1700, with additions of the 1760s, although the estate was bought by the Cheapes of Rossie in 1669. Kinloch House is a contemporary of Rossie, but was altered in 1859 and again in 1921–3 by Sir Robert Lorimer's extensions.

Auchtermuchty is remembered in the Scottish poem 'The Wife of Auchtermuchty', allegedly written by James V.

AUCHTERTOOL

Auchtertool, once a village of cottars and weavers within its own parish, was anciently known as Milntoun on the lands of Ochtertuill belonging to the bishopric of Dunkeld, to which it had been gifted by David I. In 1592 by the Act of Annexation the village and its parish lands were assumed by the Crown and James VI conferred them on John Boswell of Balmuto House, a fifteenth- and sixteenth-century dwelling (reconstructed at various times) south of the village. By the eighteenth century most of the parish belonged to the Earl of Moray who exploited the quarry rights.

The parish church dates from its reconstruction of 1833 and has later additions. The churchyard has relics of the earlier site; one tabletomb shows Auchtertool's minister David Martin (fl. 1636) carved in clerical dress. The former Auchtertool manse, now Candle-ford House (1812), shows how opulent the lifestyle of nineteenth-century rural clergy in Fife could be.

Auchtertool House dates from the early nineteenth century, but in history the village was dominated by the (ruined) mansion of Hallyards. Fife legend avers that the bishops of Dunkeld had a 'palace' on the Hallyards site, with Bishop William de Sanct Claro (Sinclair) a regular visitor. The bishop earned his name of the 'Fechting Bishop' from Walter Bower's account of him repulsing a hostile English force which landed at Donibristle around 1310.

Whether this was all true or not Hallyard's first documented proprietor was Sir James Kirkcaldy of Grange, Scotland's Lord High Treasurer, who expanded his Auchtertool lands by paying George Crichton, Bishop of Dunkeld, a sum of money for church decoration. By the early seventeenth century the barony of Auchtertool was acquired by Sir Andrew Skene of Auchrie and Hallyards became that family's dwelling. On the death of the estate's direct heir, General Philip Skene, the policies were acquired by the Earl of Moray who changed the name to Camilla.

National events gave Auchtertool some moments of fame. It is said that when James V was en route for Falkland Palace, after his defeat by the English force of Sir Thomas Wharton at Solway Moss in November 1542, he rode through the village to rest at Hallyards. A short while later James was dead. Again in 1715, when the Jacobites were being rallied by John Erskine, Earl of Mar, to support the claims of Prince James Francis Edward Stewart for the British throne, Auchtertool welcomed the Fife gentry congregating at Hallyards. And they also saw the Jacobites rally at Burntisland under Brigadier William Mackintosh to taunt the Hanoverian men-o'-war in the Forth.

Auchtertool was also the locus of a famous duel. On 26 March 1822, Sir Alexander Boswell (b.1755), son of James Boswell, the friend and biographer of Dr Samuel Johnson, was mortally injured by a pistol shot delivered by James Stuart of Dunearn. It appears that Boswell had lampooned Stuart in the political journal *The Sentinel* and Stuart had 'called him out'. Boswell died the next day and Stuart was acquitted of murder.

Auchtertool was later famous for its nineteenth-century distillery which produced ales, porter and table beers for the London market.

BACKMUIR OF NEW GILSTON

The village of Gilston – 'the Gilliee' toun o' Lundin' – is within a medieval moorland and the parish of Newburn, formerly Drumeldry. The lands were probably Crown-held in the reign of Malcolm III. Developed as an area of farm steadings, the lands fell to the ownership of the Lundins of that Ilk up to the eighteenth century, whereupon they had various subsequent owners. Gilston House is a late nineteenth-century mansion.

BAINTOWN

Hamlet in the old parish of Kennoway, within the medieval estates of the earls of Rothes. Associated with local agriculture, shoemaking, brewing and coarse linen trades.

BALBIRNIE MILLS (see: AUCHMUTY)

BALCURVIE

Once formed part of the barony of Durie within the parish of Markinch. Now linked with Windygates and sports a mansion house, pre-1854. The adjacent location of The Temple suggests lands once held by the Knights Templar.

BALDINNIE

Scattered hamlet in Ceres parish. Inhabitants once associated with local farm steadings and linen weaving. Formerly supported its own school.

BALLINGRY

Taking its name from its former parish, Ballingry, the modern village had its roots in a district called Lochoreshire with its motte and tower castle of Inchgall by Loch Orr. Once pronounced 'Bingry', the village began as a pastoral hamlet of tenants dependent on Lochore Castle which local tradition says was founded by Sir Duncan de Lochore in the reign of Malcolm IV (1153–65). By Robert the Bruce's reign (1306–29) it had fallen to the de Vallence family who held it up to the marriage of a daughter of James de Vallence to Sir Andrew Wardlaw of Torrie; thence the Wardlaw family held it into the mid-seventeenth century. Sir Andrew was the elder brother of cardinal priest (without title) Walter Wardlaw, Bishop of Glasgow (1367), and father of Bishop Henry Wardlaw of St Andrews. Lochore Castle (Inchgall) ruins date from the fourteenth and fifteenth centuries on a known twelfth-century site. The ruins are a feature of the Lochore Meadows Country Park, 1969–70, reclaimed from an area polluted by mine workings. Ownership of a greater part of the Ballingry area fell to John, Earl of Rothes, around 1627.

Modern Ballingry is made up of miners' housing of three development phases c.1900–47, linking Ballingry with Lochore, Crosshill and Glencraig. The parish church dates from 1831 in its main block, with seventeenth-century relics and eighteenth-century headstones in the graveyard. The manse dates from 1852. Local tradition has it that a church was founded here by missionaries sent from Lochleven by St Serf in the sixth century.

Sir Walter Scott mentions Ballingry Church in *The Abbot* (1820); Scott was a frequent visitor to the area from Blairadam, and his eldest son Walter married the heiress Jane Jobson of Lochore House, a mansion of around 1790.

Near to Ballingry is Benarty Hill, with its prehistoric fort. This gave rise to local traditions of a tribal settlement that was attacked by the Romans. Writing in the late 1790s, the Rev. Thomas Scott of Ballingry averred that it was here that Governor Gnaeus Julius

Agricola's *IX Hispania* Legion (from Pannonia, modern Hungary) came to grief in AD 82 when Domitian was emperor. Benarty House dates from 1830–35.

BALMALCOLM

Set within the old parish of Kettle, Balmalcolm was an eighteenth-century weaving village which gave way to agricultural pursuits. The area was particularly known for its dowlas (a coarse linen cloth) and linen window blinds. As the lands of Kettle are first mentioned in an 1166 charter of Malcolm IV to Duncan, Earl of Fife, on his marriage to Malcolm's neice Ada, Balmalcolm, stretched along the A92 Cupar–Glenrothes road, is deemed 'Malcolm's Town'. Today it is the home of the vegetable packers Kettle Produce.

BALMERINO

Balmerinoch, Balmerinauch, Balmarinac and a dozen other spellings were used in the chronicles of the original developers of this village, the Cistercian monks of the Abbey of the Blessed Virgin and St Edmund the Confessor, Balmerino. The abbey was founded around 1227 by Ermengarde, second wife and widow of William the Lion, and her son Alexander II, with monks from the Cistercian mother house of St Mary's Abbey, Melrose (1136) under Abbot Alan. Ermengarde, it is said, often visited the abbey 'for the benefit of her health', on the lands she bought for the Cistercians from Adam de Stawel of Cultra, Balmerino and Ardint. The dowager queen was buried before the high altar of the abbey on her death in 1233. The ruins of the abbey and the *c.* fifteenth-century Abbot's House are in the care of the National Trust for Scotland to whom they were presented by the Earl of Dundee in 1936.

The abbey flourished as an important agricultural landlord, establishing the dependent hamlet, granges, orchards (destroyed in the infamous gale of 1879) and harbour. In December 1547 the abbey was attacked by the English forces of Thomas Wyndham, and the Reformers perpetrated some damage in June 1559. Much of the abbey must have been habitable, though, as Mary, Queen of Scots stayed here during Fife visits of 1564–5. During the period 1603–07, the abbey was erected into a temporal lordship for Sir James Elphinstone, created Lord Balmerino.

Arthur, the 6th Lord Balmerino (b.1688) caused his eponymous village and parish to assume national, if notorious, prominence. A distinguished Jacobite, exiled for his part in the 1715 rebellion, Lord Balmerino joined Prince Charles Edward Stewart at Holyrood during the rebellion of 1745. Balmerino was taken prisoner at the Battle of Culloden on 16 April 1746. He was tried for treason, found guilty and executed on Tower Hill, London, on 18 August 1746. The title died with him as did the Jacobite cause he promoted.

The village of Balmerino developed a core south of the abbey on the western slopes of Scurr Hill by the Tay. In time Balmerino linked, along with the hamlet of Kirkton of Balmerino, with the settlement of Bottomcraig by Naughton House of 1793. A garden was made in the remains of sixteenth-century Naughton Castle, largely built by the Crichtons of Naughton and demolished in 1790. Local legend sites a castle here from the thirteenth century.

Balmerino Parish Church dates from 1811 with a manse of 1816; this church replaced a foundation of 1595 at Kirkton of Balmerino. The David Scrymgeour-Wedderburn Memorial Square (1948) lies just to the south of the abbey ruins, and the village sports a mixture of eighteenth- and early nineteenth-century (pantiled) houses. By the eighteenth century Balmerino harbour, the former site of the monks' quays, was busy with corn and lime shipments to Dundee, with fishing craft too into the 1900s. Up to 1915 paddle-steamers visited Balmerino, a regular caller being the vessel *Bonnie Dundee*, disgorging excursionists bound for the tearoom and the now defunct eighteenth-century Balmerino Inn.

BALMULLO AND LUCKLAWHILL

Balmullo, in old Leuchars parish, was within that portion of land granted by William the Lion to the De Quincys, earls of Winchester. It developed as an agricultural and flax-weaving community with famous market gardens. It sits at the foot of Lucklaw Hill. Today it is a popular dormitory village. The redstone quarry at the side of Lucklaw Hill is a landmark for miles. Lucklawhill was once the centre of a small estate.

Two houses in the neighbourhood are worthy of mention: Pittormie dates from 1764 with additions of 1867, and sits within an area of soft fruit cultivation. Pitcullo has a sixteenth-century heart and was restored from a ruin in 1971. Writing in 1792, the Leuchars minister, the Rev. Kettle, noted that Pitcullo estate was a pioneer in agricultural improvements and had much of the finest timber in Fife as well as extant medieval hedgerows.

BALONE

Now a housing development area, Balone began as a hamlet dependent upon the estate of the same name: Bylone in the eighteenth century and Ballone in the nineteenth. In 1627 it belonged to Sir John Preston of Penicuik. Hereabouts, too, was one of the granges belonging to the Augustinian priory of St Andrews; the grange was rebuilt by Prior James Haldenstone (*c.* 1370–1443), who probably refurbished priory property at Pilmore, Seggie and Kynmonth at the same time.

BARNYARDS

Hamlet in the old parish of Kilconquhar, to the north of the mother village of Kinconquhar. It was an agricultural community in history.

BINNEND

Dependent at one time on the estate of The Binn, owned in the eighteenth century by the Aytons of Inchdairny.

BLAIRBURN

Acreage of the village once held by the monastery of St Serf, thereafter Culross Abbey. Blair Castle, by Blairburn, is an early nineteenth-century house; it became a convalescent home for miners as a memorial to Charles Carlow (1848–1923), erstwhile chairman and managing director of the old Fife Coal Co. Dunimarle Castle is a castle-villa dating from 1839–45. To the west are ruins thought to incorporate part of a medieval castle; legend has it that Dunimarle, once Castlehill, was the scene of the murder of Lady Macduff and her two sons. To the south is St Serf's Episcopal Chapel, built in 1870.

BLAIRHALL

North of Culross in the old parish of Culross, developed to house miners of the colliery founded in 1911. The Blairhall laird's house dates from the seventeenth century and was the birthplace of Sir William Bruce of Kinross.

Sir William Bruce, born around 1630, is something of a local hero in Fife history. Hailed as the originator of the profession of architecture in Scotland, he was leader in new garden designs of his time. Bruce travelled in both England and the Continent studying architectural styles. By 1660, following his association with the intrigues surrounding the Restoration of Charles II, he became Clerk of the Bills and was created a baronet in 1668. In 1671 he became King's Surveyor in Scotland, the year he was commanded by Charles II to prepare 'plans for a sweeping reconstruction of Holyrood Palace'.

This work gave him great cachet among the Fife nobility who jockeyed to get his advice on the expansion and reconstruction of their own mansions. Thus Bruce's hand and 'consultancy' is to be seen at Raith House (1693–96), Abbotshall parish; Leslie House, 1667–74; Wemyss Hall (now Hill of Tarvit), 1696; Craighall, 1617–99, at Ceres; and Melville House, 1697–1703, by Ladybank. Bruce also enlarged Balcaskie House for himself during 1668–74, and 'completed' his great-grandfather's castle of Earlshall. Bruce's title 'of Kinross' came from his purchase of the estate of Kinross and the building of the extant mansion there during 1685–90. Bruce died in 1710.

BLEBO CRAIGS

Blebo Craigs lies west of St Andrews on the slopes of Clatto Hill, within the old parish of Kemback. Once there were spinning mills in the vicinity at Blebo Works and Blebo Mills and some thirty sandstone quarries. In the 1720s lead was mined at Milton of Blebo, and lead was refined and exported to such places as Holland for around thirty years. Coal and lime were both worked here, but proved too expensive to extract for a sustained industry. Blebo Mill was a water- and steam-powered spinning mill operated by James and Henry Walker.

Blebo estate – once Blabolg – belonged to the Earl of Douglas in the reign of David II (r.1329–71), and was later apportioned by the monarch to the Abbey of Dunfermline. By the late fourteenth century the property had been acquired by the Traill family, a denizen of whom was Walter Traill, Bishop of St Andrews (1384–c.1400). The Traills held the property until 1649 when it was purchased by the Bethunes, who held it for over 200 years.

Blebo House is an early nineteenth-century edifice with block wing and round entrance tower of 1903. Today the village retains its character core as a nineteenth-century vernacular hamlet but has seen much modern building as a place of retirement and a dormitory for St Andrews.

BOARHILLS

This vernacular hamlet of pantiled cottages, some rubble-built with new houses in old farm steadings, lies off the A918 St Andrews to Crail road on a winding thoroughfare that leads to the sea and the old fishing havens. At Chesterhill the first lifeboat station in these parts was built (1865). This whole area was within the *Cursus Apri Regalis* – 'the run of the wild boar' – in medieval times, where prelate and noble hunted the local fauna with equal gusto. The village has a primary school building of around 1815, with additions of 1931. Boarhills Church is set apart in the fields alongside the A918 and dates from 1866–7.

Nearby Kenlygreen House, on the Kenly Burn, was designed by the Adam brothers and dates from around 1790, with seventeenth-century Kenly Green doocot across the burn; this was restored in 1987. Nearby are two interesting bridges, the Kenly Bridge of 1793 and the early sixteenth-century Peekie Bridge bearing the arms of the Hepburn family. Farms in the area exhibit features of past architectural life from horsemills to cart sheds.

In the neighbourhood of Kenlygreen House are hillocks, one of which may be the lost castle of Draffan, which appears in local lore as a fortress of Norse raiders. Here too was sited the now vanished episcopal country 'palace' of Inchmurdo, a bolt-hole for the medieval bishops of St Andrews. Some historians aver that the Kenly Green doocot was constructed from Inchmurdo stone after the Reformation.

BONNYBANK

Hamlet on the A196 Windygates to Cupar road in the old parish of Kennoway and within the medieval estates of the earls of Rothes. Although the hamlet has an agricultural background in history, it was also associated with the coarse linen trade and was linked with its close neighbour Baintown, 'Baneton' in the early nineteenth century.

BORELAND

Set along the B929, east of Kirkcaldy, this village developed from a
hamlet for colliers in 1756. Coal was mined in this area from around
1490 when the mineral revenues were drawn on behalf of the Earl of
Orkney.

BOW OF FIFE

A cluster of houses on the A91 Auchtermuchty to Cupar road at its
bisection with the road to Letham. The disused Monimail Free
Church of 1897–8 is a landmark; behind the church is a manse of
around 1845 relating to an earlier foundation. Writing in the 1790s
the minister of Monimail, the Rev. Samuel Martin, had this to say:
'Whether this uncommon name [Bow of Fife] is taken from a bend-
ing of the road, as some suppose, or, as others, from the meetings of
the farmers in old times, to fix the prices of grain (the bolls being
pronounced bows) cannot be determined. It has been thought, that
this spot is nearly the centre of Fife: this is also offered as the reason
of the name' (i.e. the focus of an estate).

BOWHILL

Bowhill is a colliery village in the old parish of Auchterderran, and
was an important medieval estate. Its modern character was entirely
shaped by the mining industry from around 1895; a flavour of its
ethos is seen around the Bowhill Library (1932), originally the
Miners' Welfare Institute. Land renewal projects are ongoing features
of the area.

BRIDGEND

Village now subsumed as a suburb of Ceres. Once had its own
school; location of the Bridgend Bleechfield mill, producing dowlas
and sheeting, and operated by J. and W. York of Pitscottie.

BROWNHILLS

Hamlet to the south-east of St Andrews on the elevated land above
the East Sands. Once linked with Easter Balmungo as part of an

estate. Medieval properties hereabouts were in the tenure of the Augustinian priory of St Andrews.

BRUNTON

Brunton, beside the Motray Water, lies in the old parish of Creich in a spur of the Ochils. These lands were once said to belong to the earls of Fife. An agricultural community in history, Brunton had some of the smallest farms in Scotland as a result of eighteenth-century feuing customs.

The monks of Lindores and Balmerino were important influences on farm development in this part of Fife. Their now vanished granges, mills, brewhouses and gardens set the tone in agriculture and horticulture in Fife's villages for decades. Because they were substantially removed from the theatre of Scotland's civil war, Fife villages like Brunton flourished. Like the hills of Largo, Kellie, Benarty and the Lomonds, the nearby Ochil foothills and Norman's Law offered open pasture for sheep and cattle, while the streams that flowed south towards the Eden and the Motray refreshed the sunny uplands. After church lands were forfeited to the Crown, poor labouring folk were turned into feuars. To be strictly fair, before the prelates of the medieval church became corrupt and self-serving, serfs found freedom, the people employment and the infirm and aged succour by the walls of the priories and abbeys.

The Rev. John Thomson, minister of Markinch, described what a Brunton farming family might be like in 1792:

> The farmer, his wife, a lad … a maid, and a boy … all worked and ate together, and all slept in the farmhouse, which consisted of one room and a kitchen … In the morning about eight [they] breakfasted on oatmeal porridge, with churned or skimmed milk, and sometimes whey. Butter was scarcely ever used, and though a few hens were kept, they and their eggs were uniformly sold. The dinner-hour was one, and the fare was always barley-broth, with plenty of cabbage or green kail, sometimes a little pork or a salt herring being added; occasionally, when there was no pork, a little butter in the broth, beef or mutton never being seen in the house. We had bread in abundance – a healthy meal, baked in the house. At night we had again porridge, or, in winter, potatoes and milk. On Sundays the master and the mistress indulged themselves in a cup of tea. I never saw or heard of spirits, wine, or even beer in the house. We made our own candles, but were more indebted in the dark nights to the splint-coal … The winter evenings were spent in the kitchen, mainly by the light

of the fire. While the women spun, the master knitted stockings, the man-servant mended his shoes and stockings ... Our stock of literature was scanty ... We had family worship every evening, the hour of which, as well as our bedtime, was a little uncertain, there being no watch or clock in the house. When the weather permitted, we regulated ourselves by the progress the seven stars made over the peat stack.

Another writer added this to flesh out another Brunton scene:

Every one who possessed a piece of land rent free was called a laird and his wife in like manner a lady. You might have seen every day a lady from the [Brunton Hills] with butter, cheese, and eggs swung over her horse in a pair of creels, and herself mounted with grave dignity above the whole, going to market with a stuff hood of large dimensions turned up only with silk on her head, and a cloak also of wool ... reckoned a piece of finery ...

Many of Brunton's old cottages had looms for the production of osnaburgs and dowlas, the coarse linen made from locally grown blue-flowered flax.

To the west of Brunton is a circumvallation of a tribal hillfort, with other vestige forts at Norman's Law – the Hill of the Norsemen – Green Craig and Black Craig and Hut Circles by Drumnod Wood.

Note: Luthrie contains the parish church (1829–32) of Creich, while Brunton was the site of a former Creich Church. The manse of Creich dates from around 1815–16. Flisk and Creich Parish Church was built in 1843.

BUCKHAVEN

Buckhaven, as Links of Buckhaven, began as a fishing village to the west of Largo Bay in the old parish of Wemyss. Today it is part of an urban sprawl merging it with Methil and Leven. For decades the village was a self-sufficient community. Writing in 1791, the Wemyss parish minister the Rev. George Gib noted: 'The fishermen in Buck-haven generally marry when young, and all of them marry fisher-mens' daughters of the same village'. Assessing the early history of the village the Rev. Gib brought to the public notice a letter in his collection written on 20 August 1778, by the Rev. Dr Harry Spens, Minister of Wemyss 1744–80 and then Professor of Divinity at St Andrews University, commenting on the village's origins. Spens wrote:

As far as I have been able to learn, the original inhabitants of Buckhaven were from The Netherlands about the time of Philip II [of Spain 1527–99; The Netherlands were a Spanish possession before 1555]. Their vessel had been stranded on the shore. They proposed to settle and remain. The family of Wemyss gave them permission. They acquired our language and adopted our dress, and for these threescore years past, they have had the character of a sober and sensible, and industrious and honest set of people. The only singularity in their ancient customs that I remember to have heard was that of a richly ornamented girdle or belt, wore by their brides of good condition and character at their marriage, and then laid aside and given in like manner to the next bride that should be deemed worthy of such an honour …

Certainly for centuries 'Buckhyne' villagers, as they were known, were considered a breed apart. Daniel Defoe described Buckhaven as 'a miserable row of cottages', while other Fifers mocked the 'fishers, land-labourers, weavers and other mechanics' for their 'clownish nature'. This was further commented upon by publisher Robert Chambers in 1828:

Their ignorance was, a good deal more than a century ago, made the subject of a grossly ridiculous and satirical pamphlet, which is still known to stall-students under the specious title of *The History of Buckhaven, comprising the Sayings of Wise Willie and Witty Eppie, and an Account of their College.* There is, moreover, preserved in the Advocates' Library, a broadside of date 1718, in which Buckhaven is represented ironically as a great seminary of learning, and a place where the elegances of life were carried to an unexampled pitch of perfection. The result of all this lampooning has been that Buckhaven is looked upon as the most uncultivated place in the country …

Chambers, a regular visitor to Fife, covered himself by noting that in his opinion Buckhaven folk were no different from other Fifers.

The Buckhaven of Spens, Gib and Chambers has long been swept away, as from the late nineteenth century it developed as a mining town which erased the old fishing village. Bowman and Co. introduced mining in 1864 and the Old Denbeath mine was sunk in the 1870s. Yet for a while Buckhaven was known for its 'Miner Fishermen', who worked in the pits in the winter and went to the fishing grounds in the summer. All the mines have now vanished.

Nevertheless the spirit of the old mining community is still extant in Buckhaven's buildings. In time a parish church was built (1899–1902), a primary school in 1907 and the former Miners' Welfare

Institute of 1924–5 became a community centre. A certain individuality was also represented in the erection of the Buckhaven Free
Church; it had originally been constructed in 1824–5 at St Andrews
as an episcopal chapel. It was dismantled and rebuilt at Buckhaven in
1870, having been brought stone by stone by sea. Today it has been
converted for secular use.

The old village of Buckhaven is remembered in this old rhyme
about Fife folk:

> The canty carles[1] of Dysart,
> The merry lads of Buckhaven,
> The saucy limmers[2] o' Largo,
> The bonnie lasses of Leven.

> [1] fellow
> [2] cheeky women

BURNSIDE

Set on the burn flowing from Lindores Loch, Burnside was a hamlet
dependent upon the abbey of Lindores. Its inhabitants probably
worked in the abbey mills, orchards and granges. In the eighteenth
century a few linen weavers lived hereabouts.

BURNTISLAND

The *portus gratiae*, or *portus salutis*, of twelfth-century medieval
monastic documents, the harbour settlement of Burntisland set at the
foot of The Binn, was in the old parish of Wester Kinghorn until the
parish took the harbour's name. Such historians as John Leighton
(1840) aver that the Romans had a naval station here.

Once in the ownership of the abbey of Dunfermline, who called
the acres 'Cunyngarland' – their rabbit warrens – Burntisland was
exchanged by the clerics with James V around 1541 and was erected a
royal burgh by James VI in 1586. James V used its sixteenth-century
quays as a naval base; these berths were remodelled in 1872–6. For
centuries, then, Burntisland enjoyed a status of great importance,
largely because of its trade with the Low Countries. At one time the
docks hummed with coal exports and bauxite imports and the town
saw the first railway ferry in the world, opened in 1850 between
Burntisland and Granton. The ferries ceased in 1952. Cromwell saw
the site as of strategic importance and captured the burgh in 1651;

and Samuel Pepys noted that Burntisland was bombarded by the Dutch fleet in 1667 during the Second Dutch War.

Today Burntisland history may be absorbed in the following locations. St Columba's Parish Church is set in East Leven St and dates from 1592–5: its squat pinnacled tower, topped with an octagonal belfry of 1749, is a landmark. This church boasts of being the first church built after the Reformation, and still exhibits the Mariners Loft from which sailors could make a discreet exit from services to suit the tide. Early village Burntisland is centred on a little church at Kirkton, rededicated to St Serf by Bishop de Bernham of St Andrews in 1246. The church was abandoned when St Columba's was ready.

Rossend Castle was the medieval 'Burntisland Castle' of Fife history, said to have been built in 1119 by the abbots of Dunfermline. Its present core dates from 1554 and its reconstruction from 1975.

Mary Somerville's House, at 30–31 Somerville Square, was named after Mary Fairfax Somerville (1780–1872), the daughter of Vice-Admiral Sir William Fairfax, one of Nelson's captains. She was a distinguished mathematician and astronomer, and a pioneer of women's education. She gave her name to Somerville College, Oxford (1879), the university's first college for women.

High Street forms the backbone of modern Burntisland, but only the eighteenth-century Star Tavern recalls earlier buildings. The

Rossend Castle

Burntisland showing the seventeenth-century fishing quays, which James V had repaired in 1541. Cromwell's ships also used the quays in 1651. Rossend Castle of 1554 sits strategically above the harbour. [*Author's collection*]

Town Hall dates from 1845–6, but Burtisland had a tolbooth in 1605. At Kinghorn Road are to be seen the villas of nineteenth-century residential Burntisland.

CADHAM (see: GLENROTHES)

CAIRNEYHILL

Delineated as a 'roadside village' in the barony and parish of Carnock, Cairneyhill evolved from around 1730 out of a smaller seventeenth-century hamlet, and has a selection of nineteenth-century vernacular houses. The church, in the main street, was constructed as a Burgher-Seceder Chapel in 1752. The village once formed part of the estate of Pitdennies, in the ownership of Sir John Halkett of Pitfirran, proprietor of Whinnyhill Colliery, and supported a modest weaving community. It is now a dormitory village of Dunfermline.

CARDENDEN

A mining village within the conglomeration of such with Auchter-derran and Bowhill, developed from 1895 in the old parish of Auchterderran. The village grew up around the mines of Dundonald and Cardenden. Its school and schoolhouse date from 1900–01. The old focal point of mid-sixteenth century Carden Tower has vanished; it stood on a rock above the Carden Burn within the Raith estate and was owned by the family of Mertyne of Medhope who were granted title by James IV in 1482. It then fell to the Crown which granted the manor, tower, mills, woods, mineral rights and village to the Mortenes and to a line of various owners including the Earl of Leven. This area was once a desolate place, the haunt of gypsies from around 1450.

CARNBEE

An elevated hamlet overlooking the Forth, Carnbee is set within its rural parish. Kellie Law (557 ft) rises to the west. Carnbee Parish Church was rebuilt during 1793–4, with interior renovations of 1854 and 1908. In pre-Reformation times it was within the benefice of the abbey of Dunfermline. Carnbee House was constructed as the manse in 1819–20. Once coal was worked in the parish which also supported corn and lint mills. The lands of Carnbee were for several centuries in the ownership of the Melville family: Sir Robert Melville acquired the property around 1309. The estate was then acquired by the Galloways, Lord Dunkeld and later fell to the Anstruthers. The mansion of Carnbee, the hub of the estate, was demolished in 1813.

CARNOCK

A small village set astride a winding Main Street, within its epony-mous old parish. A roofless pre-Reformation church of around 1250 in origin stands off Main Street; once it was the property of the Red Friars' (Trinitarians) Hospital at Scotlandwell, gifted to them by Bishop David de Bernham of St Andrews. Repaired and remodelled in 1602, at the call of Sir George Bruce, holder of the barony. Later work was done in 1641 and 1772 but the church was abandoned in 1840 at the institution of a new parish church built 1838–40 and renovated 1894.

In the kirkyard is buried the Rev. John Row (1568–1646) who was minister of the old parish church 1592–1646. Row, from a distinguished family of Reformers, was part author of the *Historie of the Kirk of Scotland from the Year 1558 to August in Anno 1637.* Carnock was once well known in Fife for the strictness of its Presbyterian discipline. For instance the Kirk Session of Carnock recorded: '1650, Dec 22. Andrew Andersone made his public repentance for carrying a load to the mill upon the last Sabbath. Likewise James Stirkie made his public repentance for hanging a dog upon the Sabbathe.'

In the eighteenth century the village was a prolific producer of barley, meal and potatoes, with several coalmines in the parish, where the Rev. Dr John Erskine of Carnock (d.1803) was a prominent mine-master. Coal was transported to the pier at Torryburn. Stone quarries provided a range of fashionable building stone. Carnock was famous for its 'polished black' monumental stone, 'white grain' and 'brown' for building. Carnock manse dates from 1742 and in 1791 Carnock employed a parochial schoolmaster at £8 6s 8d (£8.34p) per annum teaching fees.

A short distance north-east of Carnock lies Luscar House, built in 1838 with extensions of 1890–01. To old Luscar House came Sir Walter Scott in June 1830 to breakfast with Adam Rolland's family – the owner himself was absent, 'arrested' by gout at Edinburgh.

CELLARDYKE

A fisher community was extant around the old creek of Skinfasthaven, Nether Kilrenny, by the 1570s. By the turn of the seventeenth century the settlement was being called Silverdykes, to be corrupted in time to Cellardyke. The land hereabouts was granted to the abbey of Dunfermline by Countess Ada de Warenne, mother of William the Lion, around 1177. By the mid-fifteenth century the acres came into the ownership of the Beatons of Balfour, and in 1578 Patrick Adamson, Archbishop of St Andrews, granted John Beaton of Balfour a charter which included 'the new seaport of Skinfasthaven'.

Cellerdyke has something of a unique feature in that near to its haven was a now vanished episcopal castle-palace, built before 1465 by Bishop James Kennedy of St Andrews. In the lee of this was anchored the Hanseatic-built episcopal barge the *Salvatour* (wrecked in 1473). By the old bathing pool, at Croma House, is the location known as the 'Cardinal's Steps', and here Cardinal David Beaton, Archbishop of St Andrews, alighted from his barge on his way to the castle-palace.

Today Anstruther Easter runs contiguous with Cellardyke. In 1883 Cellardyke was disjoined from the parish of Kilrenny, to evolve its own parish church in Toll Road. The first Cellardyke Town Hall was built in 1624; the foundation stone of a new Town Hall was laid in 1882. Cellardyke retains its atmosphere of an old-fisher village of independent folk with their own dialect and superstitions. The building of the new harbour at Anstruther helped kill off Cellardyke as the home of the local fleet.

CERES

Once a linen-weaving village, Ceres enters reliable recorded history as a burgh of barony around 1620. Early owners of the land hereabouts were the ancestors of the Scotts of Balwearie who acquired the property by marriage into the De Syres family, and who held title from the reign of William I (the Lion) to 1599 when the properties were disponed to the Kininmonths; in the reign of Charles I the lands were secured by Sir Thomas Hope of Craighall, King's Advocate, and thereafter to a whole range of purchasers as the lands were split up.

Craighall

The seventeenth-century Bishop Bridge abutting St John's Masonic Lodge of 1765, Ceres, by the village green. Ceres was made burgh of barony in 1620. [*Staralp*]

Ceres was once famous for its two fairs, for the sale of wool, corn, horses and cattle, on 24 June and 20 October. Local legend has it that they were held as a privilege by Ceres folk because at the Battle of Bannockburn (1314), Sir Robert Keith, Great Marishal of Scotland, Baron Struthers, joined the standard of Robert the Bruce, with Ceres men under the Lord of Craighall. Craighall mansion (1697–9) was demolished in 1955, and fifteenth-century Struthers Castle was abandoned in the early eighteenth century.

The pre-Reformation church of St Ninian at Ceres belonged to the provostry of St Mary's, Kirkheuch, St Andrews. The present church was built on its site in 1806. The churchyard still contains the seventeenth-century Lindsay Vault and that of the earls of Crawford. The unmarked grave of Patrick, Lord Lindsay of the Byres, is hereabouts; he figured in the abdication story of Mary, Queen of Scots.

The present church was built on the medieval site during 1805–06. The parish school at Ceres dates from 1835–6, with additions of 1961, while the schoolhouse dates from 1850; even so the village heritors supported a school here from the 1630s. Ceres Main Street offers a range of eighteenth- and nineteenth-century properties inter-larded with modern.

At the centre of the village, which still has a village green, stands the seventeenth-century Weight House, which served as a burgh tolbooth and as a venue for the barony courts. The 'jougs' – a hinged collar chained to the wall – still remain as an example of summary justice for miscreants on market days. The building was gifted to the Central and North Fife Preservation Society who founded the Fife Folk Museum in this and adjoining buildings in 1968. The museum offers an overview of local history as well as Fife socio-economic activities down the ages. The garden gallery overlooks the Ceres Burn and the seventeenth-century Bishop's Bridge. Over this bridge, says local tradition, the carriage of Archbishop James Sharp rattled back in 1679 only minutes away from his assassination at Magus Muir. Nearby is St John's Masonic Lodge of 1765, restored in 1964. Near the museum in the High Street is the figure known as 'The Provost'. He sits 'merry as a Toby jug' within his alcove and is local sculptor John Howie of Sauchope's conception of a church provost, the Rev. Thomas Buchanan, the last holder of the office. Set beneath the statue is a Howie panel said to commemmorate Bannockburn. Ceres Games, which are still held annually, are thought to have derived from the celebrations after the victory at Bannockburn.

CHANCE INN

On the Great Road network between Forth and Tay, the village in the old parish of Ceres was established in the early 1800s. In an assessment of Fife placenames written in 1924, the Rev. Dr John Campbell wrote that the village was once 'Change Inn', a change-house where fresh horses could be obtained for onward coach journeys. Change Inn declined when the main road to and from Cupar was realigned.

CHAPEL

A hamlet now incorporated into the north-west of modern Kirkcaldy.

CHARLESTOWN

Charlestown remains a fine example of an early planned seaport village laid out in a long rectangle round a green. In the old parish of

Dunfermline, Charlestown was founded in 1756 by Charles Bruce, 5th Earl of Elgin and 9th of Kincardine (1732–71), and the dwellings are arranged in the form of his initials 'C. E.'. From its inception the village was meant to be self-sufficient enough to create an environment of employment and leisure for the workers and their families. Its industry was centred on the working of nearby deposits of limestone processed in fourteen kilns; nine built 1777–8, and five in 1792. The resultant product was used for building and in agriculture, particularly to 'sweeten' soil, to use as a flux in glass and iron production and for mortar in the construction of such as Dundee docks and Perth's townhouse.

The limestone was carried from quarry to kiln via the horse-drawn tramway known as the Elgin Railway; this was replaced by the lines of the North British Railway but has long been lifted. The harbour was constructed in two phases, 1777–8 and in the nineteenth century. The works ceased in 1956.

Charlestown school was built in 1780 and the Sutlery (village shop) survives as a key location as well as the Old Granary of 1792, and Queen's Hall erected in 1887 to commemorate Queen Victoria's Golden Jubilee.

CHARLOTTETOWN

A small early nineteenth-century village.

CLUNY

Once this part of the parish of Kinglassie was known as Gaytmyl-schire in the ownership of the abbey of Dunfermline. The lands of Cluny were first gifted by Sybilla, Queen of Alexander I, to the Benedictines of Dunfermline, but were long in the possession of the Wemyss family. Records show that in 1538 James V united Cluny with the barony of Pittencrieff as a gift to Patrick Wemyss for services to the Crown in France.

COALDEN

A village in Kinglassie parish, once within the estate of Cluny.

COALTOWN OF BALGONIE

Part of the old parish of Markinch. Once its colliery was the main supplier of coal to inland and north Fife and was a property of the Earl of Leven; local legend has it that coal was mined here from the twelfth century. This is not a far-fetched assertion as a lease of 1291 from the owner of Pittencrieff allowed Radulphus de Grenlaw, Abbot of Dunfermline, and his chapter to mine coal 'wherever they may wish' on his estate. Incidentally, when Enea Silvio Piccolomini, later Pope Pius II, visited in the reign of James I (1405–37), he noted in one of his letters, how 'the poor at the church doors received from alms pieces of stone, with which they went away contented, and burnt in the place of wood'.

The colliers of Coaltown of Balgonie were the successors of a distinct class of Fife village folk. From feudal times Fife colliers had been treated as *adscripti glebae*, bondsmen, who were sold 'in a state of slavery' by coalmine owners when they disposed of land and mineral rights. This practice existed until 1775 when an Act was passed that colliers, coal-bearers and salters were not to 'be bound to work in [mines, salt works] in any way different from common labourers'. All were to be set free from such bondage on the day the Act received the royal assent of George III.

The Act did not apply to any still apprenticed to mine owners. Writing in 1895 Sheriff A. J. G. Mackay noted that when he was researching for his book on Fife there was 'within the memory of men now living' collieries that employed women and children as coalheavers, working in inhumane conditions. Fife village women and children (under twelve) were relieved of such work by the Earl of Shaftesbury's Act of 1842. Wages, too, went up as a consequence of this legislation, noted Sheriff Mackay, who continued 'the [Fife] collier who, a century ago, received only 7s to 8s [35p–40p] a-week, now can earn an average wage from 3s and 6d to 4s and 6d [roughly 17–22p] a-day'.

The village of Coaltown of Balgonie was originally built to house collier families. A water-engine to clear the workings was set up in 1731 by Alexander, Earl of Leven. Today the village contains a core of late Victorian terraced cottages. Sited here is one of the best early fifteenth century tower-houses in Scotland. Balgonie Castle was built around 1400 by Sir John Sibbald and was the home of General Sir Alexander Leslie (*c.*1580–1661, 1st Earl of Leven) who became leader of the Protestant army of the Solemn League and Covenant. In 1706 the 3rd Earl of Leven added to the site above the River Leven. In 1716 Rob Roy McGregor captured the castle from the Hanoverian General William Cadogan. Long neglected, the castle was restored from the 1970s.

COALTOWN OF BURNTURK

The barony of Burnturk, within the old parish of Kettle, was a portion of the properties of the earls of Fife, and was assumed as Crown lands at the forfeiture of Murdoch, Earl of Fife, son of Robert, Duke of Albany. Murdoch was executed by order of James I in 1425 when the Fife title was attainted. Thereafter James I apportioned Burnturk to various tenants until in 1501 the lands were bought by Walter Heriot of Lathane and chartered to him by James IV. Thus Burnturk became a full barony with a mansion and remained in the Heriot family until 1566. By the 1890s it was owned by Alexander Lawson, a prosperous maufacturer of handloom fabrics. Burnturk was known for its freestone, limestone, ironstone and coal.

COALTOWN OF CALLANGE

With North and South Callange, in history Coaltown of Callange formed a scattering of mining hamlets within an agricultural setting in the parish of Ceres. Limestone was also mined in the area.

COALTOWN OF WEMYSS

Set along the A995 Kirkcaldy–Methil road, the village was once made up of West and East Coaltown within the ancient parish of Wemyss. When the Wemyss Coal Co. expanded activities in 1860 the two villages amalgamated as a 'model mining village'. At the gates of Wemyss Castle there is a row of 1890s miners' housing.

COLINSBURGH

This 'roadside village' was founded in 1682 and named for Colin, 3rd Earl of Balcarres (1652–1722); it was elevated to a burgh of barony in 1686. A friend of James VII and II, the earl refused to accept the accession of William III and supported the rising of John Graham of

Claverhouse, Viscount Dundee; he was imprisoned for his activities. He was also engaged in the plot of Sir James Montgomery of Skelmorely to restore James. He fled to exile in Holland in 1690 where he wrote *An Account of the Affairs of England relating to the Revolution* (1688), and remained in exile until 1700. Thereafter he was pensioned by Queen Anne and supported the Treaty of Union. The earl ratted once more on his benefactors and supported the 1715 Jacobite rising; he surrendered when the uprising collapsed.

Balcarres House was the seat of the Lindsays from the late sixteenth century after Judge John Lindsay, Lord Menmuir, bought the property. The 3rd earl enlarged the house which was remodelled 1838–43.

Colinsburgh Parish Church dates from 1843–4 and the Town Hall from 1894–5, with a range of terraced houses of the eighteenth and nineteenth century. A library was founded here by public subscription in 1899. The village once sponsored a flourishing weekly market and two annual fairs to sell cattle. It was also known for its currying-work, in which tanned leather was dressed.

COLLESSIE

In medieval times this old weaving village was once known as Kirkton of Collessie and was a conspicuous elevation in a marshy area rich in peat formerly cut by the heritors the Abbots of Lindores. Here in the Howe of Fife was to be found Rossie Loch, drained in 1740 for pastureland. To the north-west at Lumquhat were the hunting grounds of David, Earl of Huntingdon, brother of William I, the Lion.

At Collessie a church, already ancient, was rededicated by Bishop David de Bernham of St Andrews on 30 July 1243. The estate of Collessie was divided many times down the centuries and apportioned into Easter and Wester areas; at one time (1450) the forestry was granted to Bishop James Kennedy of St Andrews. The Crown administered the estate from time to time, but Wester Collessie fell to the Kinloch family. Sir Alexander Kinloch built Cruive Castle as the centre of the barony.

Easter Collessie (also called Hallhill) enters recorded history as Crown land, which was often given as life-rent holdings to court dignitaries. In 1507, for instance, James IV bestowed them on William Cuming of Inverlochy, Marchmont Herald. By 1539 the property had been acquired by Henry Balnavis, erstwhile Secretary of State who as a prominent supporter of the Scottish Reformation was implicated in the murder of Cardinal David Beaton. Balnavis' properties were confiscated for his activities by Queen Regent Marie de Guise-Lorraine.

Long before Collessie developed as a medieval village, the area south of Kinloch House, built in 1859 by Charles Kinnear on an earlier seventeenth-century mansion site, was a prominent early settlement location now damaged by modern pipe-laying. Here archaeologists found evidence of a settlement of the late Neolothic to Early Bronze Age period; eight different types of pottery sherds found suggested a long-extant settlement of tribesmen who made the hills and marshes around Collessie their home and hunting grounds.

The near presence of the River Eden to the south of Collessie would suggest that the village's most early inhabitants were cousins of those who inhabited the settlements at Tentsmuir, for an early pattern of prehistoric villages follows the line of the Eden as settlers moved along its banks in search of new dwelling areas.

Collessie was once a good village in which to study the development of the rural cottage. It is doubtful if many cottages now extant in Fife are older than the early reign of James VI, say 1567–1603, while fewer are directly traceable to the reign of Queen Anne (1702–14).

In the mid-1860s Collessie was distinctive still for thatched houses, and retains a collection of seventeenth- and eighteenth-century features. The extant parish church dates from 1838–9 but incorporates earlier aspects. The graveyard includes seventeenth-century monuments. One inscription records the local opposition to burials in churches favoured by the medieval church:

DEFYLE NOT CHRISTS KIRK WITH YOVR CARRION
A SOLEMNE SAIT FOR GODS SERVICE PREPARD
FOR PRAIER PREACHING AND COMMVNION

Next to the church is the former manse (The Glebe) begun in 1796, while the schoolhouse dates from 1846. A property associated with Collessie is Melville House, built for George, 1st Earl of Melville and President of the Privy Council 1697–1703.

COMRIE

Comrie lies on the A907 out of Dunfermline. The mansion of Comrie castle lies just north of Blairhall.

COULTRA

Hamlet in Balmerino parish, in whose environs are prehistoric workings. Once known as Cultrach, Coultra was the feudal privilege of Henry de Reuel, at the behest of William the Lion. There was possibly a now vanished Culdee chapel here. De Reuel's properties were absorbed by the Abbey of Balmerino, which thereafter feued them to various parties.

COWDENBEATH

There was a barony of Beath in the early Middle Ages belonging to the Augustinian Canons of Inchcolm who held it into the sixteenth century and sponsored a chapel at Cowdenbeath. The Benedictines of Dunfermline Abbey also had land rights hereabouts, and after the Reformation the whole fell to secular hands including Anne of Denmark, wife of James VI from 1593. The Earl of Morton and others mined coal here from the early seventeenth century.

Cowdenbeath developed its modern form from around the 1870s as a mining community out of a former agricultural medieval hamlet of Coudon-baith; it was made a burgh in 1890. Of Cowdenbeath's various churches that of Beath is the oldest extant reflecting the name of the 1643 parish. Cowdenbeath Parish Church dates from 1892–3; this is an 1835 replacement of a church used 1640–1808. The Town Hall dates from 1904–06 and there was a parochial school from the eighteenth century.

CRAIGROTHIE

As with so many villages in north-east Fife, Craigrothie is set within a historical landscape that has been important since medieval times. Set on the Craigrothie Burn the village was once home to families of weavers. Well into the twentieth century the flax crop was an important part of the rural economy; a corn mill also contributed to the latter. Thereafter the village became an agricultural community.

The village was given its extant form by the eighteenth century, particularly when the ford for the main road to Cupar was given a bridge. A village school was opened in 1833 to replace one of 1806, and reopened anew in 1907. A village hall of 1975 replaced an old school building used as a hall from 1908. Craigrothie House was the home of the Gourlays, who feued the mill lands of Craigrothie from the eighteenth century.

Craigrothie has been touched historically too, with the life and times of three properties:

Scotstarvit Tower was constructed for the Inglises of Tarvit around 1500. This tower house was extended by Sir John Scott of Scotstarvit, who bought the property in 1611. The tower was abandoned in 1696 and Sir John's descendant, the Duchess of Portland, sold the estate to Oliver Gourlay of Craigrothie House; thereafter it was acquired by Colonel Wemyss of Wemysshill House, now known as Hill of Tarvit Mansion. Scotstarvit is administered by Historic Scotland.

Struthers Castle, now ruined, was built in the early sixteenth century for the Lindsays of the Byres and has witnessed the pageant of north-east Fife history. This land belonged to the Ochter-Struthers in the twelfth century, who probably had an earlier home here, and at the castle Charles I was entertained in 1651; two years later the castle was occupied by Cromwell's troops.

The Sharps bought Wemysshill House in 1904 and commissioned Sir Robert Lorimer to enlarge the house and lay out the gardens. The whole became Hill of Tarvit Mansion, and has been administered by the National Trust for Scotland since 1949.

CRAIL

The village heart of Crail is formed around two parallel streets; the continuation of Westgate, High Street and Marketgait, to the north, and Nethergate West and Nethergate East to the south. Both linked with the now vanished castle, a stronghold of the early Scottish kings. Thus the earliest part of Crail developed from the hamlet outside the castle then around the aforementioned streets from the twelfth to the fourteenth century. Robert the Bruce granted Crail a charter making it a royal burgh in 1310, which was confirmed by Robert II in 1371, and again by Mary, Queen of Scots in 1553 and Charles I in 1653. Of these dates we can be reasonably certain, but Crail was deemed famous before that. Writing in 1840 John Leighton noted: 'So early as the ninth century, [Crail] is said to have had commercial intercourse with [what became] the Netherlands'. Local legend has it that Constantine I may have ridden out of the early castle to be killed by an invading Danish army around 877 at the

Crail harbour around 1840, showing the late seventeenth-century Custom House, the fisher quays and Shoregae leading to the village and castle hill above. [*Author's collection*]

battle of Inverdufatha. Certainly Constantine's Cave and the Danes' Dyke at Fife Ness recall these local traditions. The early medieval cross-slab at the parish church and the Sauchope Stone, now at a site in St Andrews Road, speak too of the village's early history. Both the castle and the parish church appear in record in the reign of Malcolm IV (1153–65), with a burgh estate in the reign of William the Lion. Interestingly the burgh long had the tradition of being a 'royal woman's burgh'; its castle and village were the marriage portions of Ada de Warrene (David I's daughter-in-law), Ermengarde, wife of William I, and Joanna, Queen of Alexander II.

David I (r.1124–53) was one of the first monarchs particularly noted as residing in Crail Castle which had its own royal chapel dedicated to Saints Rufus and Maelrubha. Throughout the early medieval period Crail was to be prominent too in ecclesiastical affairs. For instance around 1207 Adam de Crail (d.1227) was elected Bishop of Aberdeen. When Ada de Warrene died in 1178 the burgh became the seat of the Sheriffdom of Fife and remained so until it was transferred to Cupar in the thirteenth century. The wealth of the medieval village of Crail came from its fisheries.

A number of key sites are important in tracing Crail's historical roots. Crail's parish church, off Marketgate, first appears on historical record in the reign of Malcolm IV and was probably founded by Ada de Warrene; its tall west tower dates from the thirteenth century. It was dedicated by Bishop David de Bernham of St Andrews in 1243 to the Celtic St Maelrubha of Applecross, but by 1517 it was known as St Mary's Collegiate Church then owned by the Cistercian nunnery of Haddington. At the Reformation it ceased to have royal patronage and its wherewithal was transferred to the burghers of Crail. The church has been altered in various eras with a major restoration in 1963.

Also in Marketgate are the tolbooth with its sixteenth-century tower and adjacent Town Hall of 1814. Nearby is the early seventeenth-century mercat cross resited and designed for Queen Victoria's Golden Jubilee in 1887; a fountain commemorates the Diamond Jubilee of 1897. Marketgate offers a range of architecture to represent Crail's burgh development.

Crail's small tidal harbour was reconstructed in 1610, repaired in 1728, had the West Pier added in 1821–8 and a rebuilt Pierhead in 1871. From the harbour Shore Street leads to the elevation where the castle stood and into the area where a castle hamlet developed into the burgh. The castle was ruinous by 1563 but adjacent was the site of the Royal Water Mill (The King's Mill), demolished in 1920. At the eastern end of the Nethergate maps show the 'remains' of the nunnery and the priory. Both of these are 'alleged' sites which some historians say were only sites of landholdings under the patronage of the Prioress of Haddington. Certainly Priory Doocot and Briery (Priory) Well recall these supposed foundations.

CREICH

The estate of Creich gave its name to the parish and was formerly property of the earls of Fife, acquired in the late fifteenth century by Sir David Beaton of Creich, a prominent courtier of James IV who rose to be Lord High Treasurer of Scotland. The Beatons remained in and out of royal service for decades. Their residence was the sixteenth-century castle of Creich, a tower-house adjoining the extant farmhouse, and originally protected on an elevation by marshland. Here too is a lectern doocot of 1723.

To the north-west of Creich, on the road to Brunton, lies in ruin the late fourteenth-century church dedicated to St Devenic, which once belonged to the abbey of Lindores, and which contained an important chapel (*sacellum*) founded by one Gilbert Straithauchin, where masses were said 'perpetually' for such souls as that of James V and his queen. A gable was added in 1621, the occasion of its last major repair. The surrounding churchyard contains interesting memorials of Creich locals. The manse of Creich dates from 1815–16. Confusingly for visitors, Creich Parish Church is at Brunton. The parish once supported (1840) one corn water mill and seven horse-driven threshing mills.

CROMBIE

By the late nineteenth century there were two villages, Crombie Point and Crombie, within the old parish of Torryburn; the former, with Torryburn itself, formed an important harbour by the eighteenth century for the onward transportation of merchandise from Dunfermline merchants to Bo'ness and thence London. Historically the land around Crombie belonged to the Anglo-Norman family of Wardlaw and was elevated into a barony; by 1537 it was in the hands of the Colvilles who retained it off and on for four centuries. The hamlet of Crombie was redeveloped to house employees at the Admiralty Laboratory of 1912; 'Garden City' whinstone-rubble housing was erected in 1915 by the then HM Office of Works.

CROSSFORD

As with many villages in this area, Crossford had links with the now defunct Royal Navy base at Rosyth. Here in the nineteenth and twentieth centuries lived MoD employees, but the village is now a dormitory, a commuter homebase for Dunfermline and Edinburgh. Local tradition has it that the village takes its name from the ford crossed by monks and their retainers travelling between Dunfermline and Culross abbeys. The medieval Kaevil estate, remembered in the present Keavil House Hotel, is worthy of mention. Once set in Crossford's busy weaving and market garden community, Keavil House is said to have evolved its name from the cavelling system of land apportionment. Nevertheless by the fifteenth century Kaevil House was a property of the Lindsays of Cawil (that is, Keavil) and remained a family home until the First World War when it was leased to the Admiralty. From 1919 to the mid-1940s Keavil belonged to the Stewarts, rubber works owners, and then to Dunfermline Burgh Council. It was developed as a hotel from the 1980s.

CULROSS

Culross remains a unique example of what a sixteenth- or eighteenth-century Scottish burgh looked like, with its small, red-pantiled houses, narrow streets and cobbled thoroughfares, meandering to meet the 1588 mercat cross, whose shaft was replaced in 1902. Within the context of looking at the roots of Fife settlements, Culross was made a burgh of barony in 1490, to be elevated to royal burgh status by James VI in 1588. But the settlement that became Culross has an interesting traditional foundation.

Here was the legendary birthplace of St Kentigern – St Mungo to Glaswegians – following his mother Princess Thenew's flight in disgrace from her father the King of Lothian's wrath. She had been cast adrift in an open boat at Aberlady, the legend recounts, and left to perish. The wind and tide miraculously brought her to shore where Culross was to develop. Her landing place was commemorated in 1503 when Glasgow's first archbishop, Robert Blackadder, set up St Mungo's Chapel. Here St Kentigern was brought up by St Serf and sent forth to spread the Gospel. Culross's importance was assured when in 1217, Malcolm, 7th Earl of Fife, founded the abbey on the hill for the Cistercian monks of Kinloss, Moray. These monks were famed for their calligraphy and illumination and the Culross Psalter is a fine example of their work. Dedicated to the Blessed Virgin, St Andrew and St Serf, the abbey fell into secular hands at the Reformation. The parish church of Culross occupies the site of the monk's choir and has been used as such since 1633; the church was modernised in 1824.

During the sixteenth century salt panning, coalmining and trade with the Low Countries were the burgh's principal activities, and the foreshore of Sandhaven ensured prosperity. One of Culross's famous products was the now rare iron baking girdle; James VI established the town hammermen's monopoly of their manufacture in 1599. Decline set in at Culross when political end economic influence moved to central and western Scotland, and the burgh was almost forgotten until the 1930s when the restoration programme began.

A flavour of Culross's development may be seen from a study of Bessie Bar's Hall, where this maltstress carried out her manufacture in the late sixteenth and early seventeenth centuries. The palace, built in 1597 and 1611 by Sir George Bruce, now includes a restored medieval garden; the Study, with its outlook tower, was used in the late seventeenth century by Bishop Leighton of Dunblane. Culross's oldest house of 1577 stands by the mercat cross; a whole range of properties are in the care of the National Trust for Scotland. The townhouse of 1626 dominates Sandhaven with its clock-tower and frontage of 1783 and houses an exhibition and video presentation telling the burgh's 400-year story.

CULTS

Properly Kirkton of Cults, the scattered school, manse and parish church gives its name to an ancient parish from the fourteenth century. In history it included the four main hamlets of Cross-gates, Walton, Cults Mill and Hospital Mill – all to the north of Cults Hill, known for its lime quarries.

Historically here were the boundaries of the old Pictish kingdom divisions of Fife, with Forthrif to the west and Fib to the east. By the 1840s most of the land belonged to the Earl of Glasgow, heir of the

Cults Parish Church, 1793, and Manse, 1795, in a late nineteenth-century engraving. Here painter Sir David Wilkie (1785–1841) was born and immortalised Pitlessie village folk in his paintings of rural life. [*Author's collection*]

heritor Lady Mary Lindsay Crawford. In 1813 Lady Mary erected Crawford Castle and Priory on the site of an old house called Crawford Lodge (1758); this became the main seat in the area. On the slopes of Waltonhill is the Crawford Mausoleum (c. 1760) erected by George, nineteenth Earl of Crawford.

The church of Cults was once a dependency of the bishopric of St Andrews, but in 1455 was desponed to the College of St Salvator by Bishop James Kennedy and later supported a theological endowment. The extant church was built in 1793. The former manse was rebuilt in 1795 and modified in 1927 after a fire. At the earlier manse of Cults was born Sir David Wilkie (1785–1841) whose father was minister of the parish for almost four decades. In 1830 David Wilkie was appointed Painter-in-Ordinary (in late sixteenth-century Scots a 'Royal Limner') to George IV, retaining office under William IV and Queen Victoria. Within the church are memorials to Wilkie's parents, the Rev. David and Isabella Wilkie. David Wilkie's paintings *Pitlessie Fair* (1804) and *The Village Politicians* (1806) offer talented representations taken from Fife 'humble rural life'.

CUPARMUIR

Cuparmuir lies across the railway from the north bank of the River Eden, while on the south bank rises the Garlie Bank, now hugged by the steep road from Cupar to Kennoway. In medieval times this was wild moorland which gave Cuparmuir an important moment in history.

In 1559 this was the site of the 'Bloodless Battle of Cupar Muir'. The army of the Queen Regent, Marie de Guise-Lorraine, under her commander James, Duke of Chatelherault and Seigneur Henry Cleutin D'Oysel, confronted that of the Protestant Lords of the Congregation, led by the Lord James Stewart and the Duke of Argyll. Urged by Lord Lindsay, D'Oysel rode from his position on Garlie Bank up to the top of Tarvit Hill. There he saw his forces were outnumbered. A bloody engagement was avoided and the pro-French Catholic army of the Queen Regent withdrew. This was to prove an important turning point in the history of the Protestant faith in Scotland.

DAIRSIE

The village of Dairsie gives its name to the old parish and its eighteenth- and nineteenth-century cottages are ribboned along a main street (A91). Once it was called Osnaburg, or Dairsie Muir. Osnaburgh was the name given to a coarse linen once traded in the village; it was a cloth originally brought from Osnaburg in Germany. It may be noted that although many of the weavers of Dairsie were employed by Cupar manufacturers there were two water-powered mills at Newmiln and Lydiamiln.

The land hereabouts was anciently held by the Dairsies of that Ilk, under the superiorship of the See of St Andrews. The Dairsies held the posts of baillies and 'admirals of the Regality of St Andrews'. By marriage the Learmonths acquired the lands of Dairsie; family legend has it they were the descendants of the celebrated Thomas 'The Rhymer' Learmonth of Ercildoune (Earlston), Berwickshire. During the reign of Charles I, the lands of Dairsie were secured by John Spottiswoode, Archbishop of St Andrews and Lord High Chancellor of Scotland, from the Lindsays of the Byres who had held them from the late sixteenth century.

The extant Dairsie Castle is a late sixteenth-century tower-house, a seat of the Learmonths, and has been reconstructed in recent times. From the thirteenth century the bishops, and after 1475 the archbishops, of St Andrews had a residence at Dairsie; probably a fortified house on the foundations of the present castle. Certainly a 'parliament' of nobles was held here in 1335 and it is said that David II spent part of his boyhood here.

St Mary's Parish Church, now disused, dates from 1621 and later; above the Renaissance door are the arms and initials of the builder Archbishop Spottiswoode – below the shield is the text *Iehovah, dilexi de corem domus tuae* (Jehovah, I have loved the beauty of thy house: from Psalm 26:8). Today Dairsie parishioners worship in the plainer former United Free Kirk (erected 1843, restored 1877) on the main street. It should be noted that there are a number of records telling of a church at Dairsie from at least the twelfth century as a gift of Arnold, Bishop of St Andrews 1159–63; this church was given to the Augustinian Priory of St Andrews in 1300. It seems that this church was the one rebuilt by Archbishop Spottiswoode. Below the castle and church is the three-arched Dairsie Bridge over the River Eden; it carries the initials and arms of the builder (around 1530), James Beaton, Archbishop of St Andrews 1522–39.

DALGETY BAY

Dalgety Bay began as a development of speculative housing on the old Donibristle Estate in 1962. Intended as a dormitory settlement for Edinburgh, the first houses were completed in 1965, with a primary school of 1969 and a new church of 1980–81. An industrial estate has developed nearby as well as a railway halt. Once the old parish of Dalgety was dependent upon the fortunes of the Fordell pit, its coal exported from St David's harbour; the hamlet that once supported the harbour became a 'lost village' when the coal (and salt) trade declined.

It is worthy of note that, writing in 1840, the historian John Leighton reported: 'An old village once existed at Dalgety, which has now been entirely removed.' The centre of the area was once the Donibristle Estate; Donibristle House is no more, but vestige wings of c.1720 remain with the derelict 1729–32 chapel and eighteenth-century stables, all forming the seat of the earls of Moray. The lands once belonged to the monks of Inchcolm, and the first castle on the site belonged to James Stewart, Lord of Doune, Commendator of Inchcolm. His son was 'the Bonnie Earl of Moray' of popular ballad, slain on the 'green' in front of Donibristle House in 1592 by the Earl of Huntly. After the murder Huntly caused Donibristle House to be burned to the ground and although it was replaced it burned down again in 1858.

Two buildings are important in the ecclesiastical history of the place: the disused Dalgety Parish Church of 1829–30 (the old manse of 1828–9 is now Ardmhor House) and St Bridget's Church. The latter was built by the monks of Inchcolm and is now made up of a later two-storey building comprising a burial vault on the ground floor and a 'laird's loft' above. The edifice was dedicated to the Irish fifth-century saint the Abbess Bridget in 1244. St Bridget's was used as a residence in the house of 1610, added to the west elevation by the Covenanting pastor Andrew Donaldson who was ejected at the restoration of episcopacy in 1661. Just outside the walls is a small stone building which acted as a watch-house against bodysnatchers. The church was deroofed in 1830.

Sir Walter Scott's knowledge of Fife gives the old parish of Dalgety a literary association. In his *A Legend of Montrose* (1819) Scott introduces Rittmaster Sir Dugald Dalgetty, a soldier of fortune, but beneath Dalgety's modern villas lie clues of an earlier age.

In recent years excavations at Dalgety Bay have revealed some interesting data about early settlements in Fife. Here in 1986 two cists were found, each containing skeletons; one was buried with a bronze dagger – nothing unusual in a Bronze Age site – but there were also the remains of the plant *Filipendula*, which the old Fife folk called meadowsweet. Archaeologists say that this fragant flower was used to flavour mead, others that the plant was a popular one in ritualistic acts, hence its presence in the grave.

Dalgety has also produced a range of Neolithic pottery, at places like Barns Farm, to indicate that the location was popular as a dwelling long before Edinburgh commuters made it their home.

Archaeological examination also shows that Dalgety's early inhabitants were fond of whelks and mussels, judging by the number of discarded shells found. Jet disc beads were also found, suggesting perhaps that old Dalgety was a place for the manufacture of primitive jewellery.

DAMS

Hamlet. Once within the medieval lands of the earls of Fife, thereafter Crown property until Kettle parish was divided into separately owned portions.

DEN OF LINDORES

Hamlet at the junction of the A983 Newburgh to Auchtermuchty, and the A913 Newburgh to Cupar roads. The lands originally belonged to the earls of Fife and subsequently became Crown lands by forfeiture. North of the Den, lying beside the A913, is Denmylne Castle, a late sixteenth-century tower-house which is recorded in history as a royal mill given to the Balfour family by James IV in 1509. It abuts a nineteenth-century farmhouse and steading. In the immediate vicinity are scattered stones which may have come from the abbey of Lindores. The Balfours of Denmylne became prominent courtiers to succeeding monarchs; interesting gravestones of the Balfours lie at Abdie Church. Denmylne was abandoned by the Balfours when the policies were sold in 1772. A famous owner of the castle was Sir James Balfour of Kinnaird, Lord Lyon King of Arms. A noted antiquarian, he collected a huge library of historical manuscripts, and was involved in the survey of the Sheriffdom of

Fife used by the cartographer Timothy Pont.

Not far from Den of Lindores lies Earnside, monastic 'Hyrne-side', whose redstone quarry on the farm of Parkside was opened to the monks of Lindores by David, Earl of Huntingdon, providing fabric for their monastery; a canal conveyed the stone to the abbey site. This area was also a royal forest and in 1451 James II allowed the Abbot of Lindores to appoint a forester. On 12 July 1298, during the struggles of the Interregnum, Sir William Wallace defeated the English army of Aymer de Valence, Earl of Pembroke, near Den of Lindores; the abbey records show that after the battle the victorious Scots tarried 'for rest and refreshment'.

DENHEAD

A hamlet within St Andrews parish (Cameron parish as from 1645); once a part of the barony of Claremont. One owner was Sir William Murray, a prominent courtier of Charles I, who created him a baronet of Nova Scotia. Here too lived the historian George Martine, secretary to the murdered Archbishop James Sharp, and author of *Reliquiae Divi Andrea: Or The State of the Venerable and Primitial See of St Andrews* (1683).

DOTHAN

Hamlet.

DRUMELDRIE

Village in the parish of Newburn, with the 1813–15 parish church of Newburn nearby. Half a mile west is the ruined church, once a Culdee chapel, which was rededicated in 1243 by Bishop David de Bernham of St Andrews. Newburn House (1818–19) is the former manse.

Today the shell of the church is a mausoleum for local familes, and the stones around testify to more prosperous days when the folk of Drumeldrie and Newburn engaged in milling, handloom weaving, shoemaking, quarrying and salmon fishing. In the west corner of the graveyard lie the Lorimers, of whom the architect Sir Robert Lorimer (1864–1929) is the most famous.

Somewhere near to Drumeldrie was the home of the 'Royal Cadger'. It was his duty to carry fish from Earlsferry to the royal palace at Falkland. In recompense for such duties he had a free house hereabouts with rights to graze a cow and a pig in the parish. The surrounding land was held in ancient times by the Benedictine abbey of Dunfermline and then by the Bishop of St Andrews, but it has long been associated with the Culdees following the land gifts of Malcolm Canmore. Nearby Balchristie estate was also a part of the ecclesiatical ownership.

These days the whole area around Drumeldrie is a mixture of scattered farms and nineteenth-century mansion houses like Lahill House (once Halhill), which belonged in an earlier form to Sir Andrew Wood of Largo, and then to the Glasgow merchants the Rintouls. Nearby Coates House was the seat of the Beatons of Creich, and Sir John Leslie (1766–1832), professor of mathematics at Edinburgh. Charleton House, with its surrounding woods named after Boer townships, was built in 1749 by John Thomson and descended to the Anstruthers of Balcaskie. Additions were made to the house in 1832 and 1906.

DRUMMOCHY

Fisher-hamlet, parish of Largo.

DUNBOG

Dunbog is a loose-knit group of habitations, the centre of a small eponymous parish once in the charge of the monks of the Order of Tiron at Arbroath Abbey. Writing in 1840, historian John Leighton noted: 'within the memory of man there was a village near the church in which a weekly market was held. The improved system of agriculture which has been introduced, having led to the enlargement of the farms, soon depopulated the village, and it has now entirely disappeared.'

Once the lands of Dunbog formed a part of the barony of Ballinbreich – by the fourteenth century in the ownership of the Abernethies of Abernethy – and passed into the hands of the de Lindsays and the de Lesleys. Sir David de Lindsay was a signatory of the Declaration of Arbroath, 6 April 1320, and fought at the Battle of Halidon Hill in 1333. By the seventeenth century the properties had fallen to the Balfours, and because Henry Balfour was attainted after the 1715 rebellion the estate was forfeit until its restoration and ultimate sale in 1766 to Sir Lawrence Dundas, through whose family it passed to the Earl of Zetland.

Dunbog House was secularised around 1578 on the site of the property of Balmerino Abbey known as the Preceptory of Gadvan; by the thirteenth century the establishment had been transferred from the abbey of Arbroath to Balmerino. Staffed by two monks (the senior as 'Prior of Dunbog') the preceptory functioned as a ministry station and was noted as being in existence by 1486; it was secularised in favour of James Beaton of Creich. The 1803–04 parish church is disused; a manse was built in 1776, while a primary school dates from 1839 and 1857.

South-east of Dunbog is Collairnie Castle, a 1581 tower-house set within a nineteenth-century steading. It was once the seat of the Balfours of Collairnie.

DUNINO

A scattered grouping of church, manse, school and private houses, Dunino is set within an eponymous parish expanded in the 1890s. A conspicuous owner of the 'lands of Denino' was Lord William Keith Douglas MP (1783–1855), brother of the Marquess of Queensbury. In the 1770s the parish supported five corn mills. The early history of Dunino is vague, some sources suggesting that it was once a hamlet around a grange owned in the twelfth century by the Augustinian priory of St Andrews; certainly the priory held tenure of land here until 1593. The extant parish church dates from 1826–7, remodelled in 1928, but records suggest that there was a chapel (*Capella de Duneynach*) here from the thirteenth century: there was a possible rededication by Bishop David de Bernham in 1240. The manse dates from 1819.

A school was established at Dunino by the early 1800s and one of the most prominent teachers employed was William Tennant (1784–1848). Tennant's most enduring work was the famous *Anster Fair* and he went on to become Professor of Oriental Languages at St Andrews University. Another famous resident of Dunino was John of Fordun (*c*.1320–84) on whose work Walter Bower the historian based his *Scotichronicon*.

The principal private estate at Dunino is Stravithie. A now vanished castle was the property of the Augustinian priory of St Andrews, but on the secularisation of the property in the sixteenth century the lands fell to Margaret Erskine, the Lady of Loch Leven, who became Mary Stewart's jailor in 1567; she subsequently gave the lands to her illegitimate son by James V, the Lord James Stewart. There followed a succession of private ownerships.

Pittarthie Castle lies in ruin to the south-west of Dunino and was originally built for James Monypenny of Pitmilly around 1580; it was bought by the Bruces around 1636 and remodelled for William Bruce of Pittarthie in 1682.

DUNSHELT

A nineteenth-century weaver's village of whinstone cottages in the parish of Auchtermuchty, once known for its cotton cloth and woollen shawls. During the eighteenth century the red pantiles used in 'improving' the thatched cottages of Falkland were custom-made in Dunshelt.

Once called Inschalt, Dunshelt was formerly within the estate of Myres Castle, the *c.* 1540 tower-house, whose owner John Scrymgeour was Master of the King's Works to James V. Local legend has it that Mary Queen of Scots often passed through the village of Dunshelt to rest at Myres during boar hunts in the surrounding marshland.

DURA DEN

A hamlet in Kemback parish which owes its foundation to David Yool in the early years of the nineteenth century to support a water-wheel spinning mill called Yoolfield. It is set in a deep wooded gorge through which flows the Ceres Burn. The yellow sandstone cliffs have preserved rich layers of fossilised aquatic life. Dura House dates from the mid-eighteenth century, with 'baronial additions' of 1861. Grove House is mid-nineteenth century and Denhall late eighteenth century.

DYSART

As with Culross, for instance, Dysart has been written about in great detail in terms of its reconstruction since 1950 and reconstruction programmes to protect housing. Pan Ha's restored housing, 1968–69, is a representative example of the National Trust for Scotland's Little Houses Scheme. Dysart's roots, however, are of interest in the context of the history of Fife villages.

The wooded gorge of Dura Den in the late 1890s. For more than a century this area, rich in geological interest, supported jute mills. [*Staralp*]

Originally the 1535 stented royal burgh of Dysart, within its eponymous parish, was a 1510 burgh of barony, a holding of the St Clairs of Rosslyn, earls of Orkney. It was admitted to the Scottish Parliament in 1594. The burgh developed from a core of three streets, centering on a loosely defined square. The Sinclairs were Anglo-Normans, descendants of William de Sancto Claro, a prominent thirteenth-century landowner, and were undoubted founders of the settlement which became Dysart. A distinguished limb of the house was Sir Henry Sinclair of Rosslyn, *panetarius Scotiae* (Chief Butler) to the court of Robert the Bruce.

From at least the mid-fifteenth century Dysart manufactured and exported salt, fish and coal, and was renowned for its nails, malting and brewing. By the mid-nineteenth century its flourishing merchant shipping trade had disappeared. It was absorbed into Kirkcaldy in 1930. Two buildings in particular are representative of Dysart's medieval life:

St Serf's church, Shore Road, is the former parish church, abandoned when the 1801–02 church was erected at townhead; it retains its landmark tower built around 1500 and now attached to ruins. The tolbooth, in High Street and Victoria Street, displays a lower part of 1576 and an upper portion of around 1617; this upper section was destroyed in a gunpowder explosion in 1656 and rebuilt 1707.

Dysart's tolbooth offers a chance to reflect on such buildings in Fife and their relevance to their communities. As local government changes have altered Fife hamlets, villages and towns considerably over the decades, village pride which developed into large burgh civic dignity is historically represented in the tolbooth, or townhouse. Here were the hubs of Fifers' public life, their wealth, their spirit, their community organisation.

Early Victorian Dysart harbour and shipyard, the scene of coal and salt shipments from the fifteenth century. The great west tower of St Serf's Church, *c.* 1500, stands in Shore Road, middle right, with Dysart House, 1755–56, to the left elevation. [*Author's collection*]

Tolbooth derives from the word *tolloneum*, meaning a stall, booth or place where all kinds of taxes and dues were collected. As in other parts of Scotland Fife folk also gave their tolbooths the role of the *preforium*, fount of justice, or council chamber, and from this developed the role too of local lock-up. In history the building, fabric and maintenance of a tolbooth was the responsibility of the local magistrates, using money from the 'common works' funds of a locality. Here too would be housed the town bell and maybe a clock. Thus tolbooths are to be found at the heart of Fife communities in the main street, or adjoining the market place. Usually Fife tolbooths were founded between the sixteenth and eighteenth centuries.

Besides Dysart's tolbooth, other fine Fife examples include: Crail, *c.* 1517 with a bell of 1520, with new work in 1598 and 1776; Culross, which is of seventeenth-century origin with building additions of 1782; Inverkeithing, seventeenth century with belfry of 1754–5 and rebuilding of 1770; Pittenweem, 1588, bell-chamber, parapet and spire of around 1630, bell, 1663; West Wemyss, built in the early eighteenth century at the call of David, 4th Earl of Wemyss.

EARLSFERRY

There are various strands of tradition associated with Earlsferry. One theory has it that Earlsferry was constituted a burgh by Malcolm III around 1057–93 at the request of Macduff, *maormer* of Fife. Ferries to the Lothians, to and from North Berwick to link the pilgrim route from St Andrews to the south, began a long time before their recognised foundation by Alexander II in 1223. We are on firmer ground too with the suggestion that Earlsferry was formerly a burgh of barony under the Abbots of Culross. Certainly Earlsferry became a royal burgh in 1541.

Above where the sea-swell batters the small islands of West Vows and Chapel Ness, at Earlsferry's western extremity, stand the remains of the Ardross hospice for the poor, travellers and pilgrims, run by the Cistercian nuns of North Berwick whose benefactor Duncan, 4th Earl of Fife, may have given his name to the ferry site. Crossing the Forth, with its heavy seas and *haar* (mist) thickest off Earlsferry, was a perilous business in medieval times and the nuns set up lamps to guide the doughty travellers. Behind the chapel lie Earlsferry Links, on which golf has been played since the sixteenth century. Beside them is The Grange, founded by the Cistercian nuns.

The house passed into the hands of the Rev. Alexander Wood, son of the famous seaman Sir Andrew Wood. The house burned down in 1860. The Earl of Mar was supposed to have held secret meetings with fellow Jacobites at The Grange during the 1715 rebellion. Over this land, too, trundled the wagons of the fish cadgers bound for the royal palace at Falkland.

A Town Hall building dating from 1864–72 is situated at Earlsferry, and the place offers a range of interesting architecture from the eighteenth and nineteenth centuries. Earlsferry was formally united with Elie in 1929.

Note: Five linked roads lead together to make up the spine of modern Earlsferry and Elie: High Street, past the Victoria Hotel opposite the church, leads to Bank Street and into Links Place, with the Golf and Marine Hotels, into Williamsburgh and across the old German Wynd into Earlsferry High Street. A mile-long strip of coast used to be four separate village communities: from east to west, Elie, Liberty, Williamsburg and Earlsferry.

EAST WEMYSS

During the eighteenth and nineteenth centuries East Wemyss, once called Castleton, was a small weaving village. In 1895 it developed as a mining village at the founding of the Wemyss Coal Co.'s Michael Colliery in 1895 – it closed in 1967. Wemyss former parish church of St Mary's-by-the-Sea, closed for worship in 1976, is said to have a twelfth-century foundation but has a core of around 1528 with a small graveyard alongside the harbour. A new parish church is situated in High Road and dates from 1936–7; a manse of 1791 stands in High Street. A primary school of 1906–08 is in School Wynd. Variously called East Wemyss, or Macduff's, Castle, the extant fourteenth-century castle (in ruins) was rebuilt in present form after Edward I's soldiers had burned it in 1306, with an extension joined to the original tower around 1530 when Sir John Colville of Ochiltree obtained the barony. It was abandoned in the early eighteenth century with a portion demolished in 1967.

EDENSTOWN

Within the old parish of Collessie, Edenstown was within lands belonging to the abbey of Lindores, whose monks exploited the abundant peat moss, a feature of the medieval landscape. The village developed in the late 1830s as an agricultural community; some of the womenfolk worked at handlooms when not needed in the fields.

ELIE

Set within an eponymous parish Elie was hewn out of the parish of Kilconquhar in 1639 and was once a purely agricultural area with the name Ailie of Ardross. A burgh of barony in 1589, its acres were once a part of the barony of Ardross in the ownership of the Dishingtons. Their ancient castle of Ardross lies in ruins and was once a baronial mansion. Elie has a long history as a seaside resort, with a harbour evolving from 1582. Elie was formally linked to Earlsferry in 1929.

Elie's parish church was built by Sir William Scott of Ardross Castle in 1639 and has a distinctive campanile of 1726. A variety of townhouses built between the sixteenth and the nineteenth centuries tell Elie's story architectually. Elie House retains a nucleus of a tower-house built by Sir William Anstruther in 1697. From mansion to convent, Elie House is now a private development.

When Elie was hardly more than a village, a royal visitor came to stay. This was James Stewart, Duke of York, who ruled Great Britain

Elie House

A popular postcard scene of Elie High Street showing the late nineteenth-century buildings which replaced earlier dwellings. The place became a burgh of barony in 1589 and incorporates the villages of Liberty and Williams-burgh. [*Staralp*]

as James II and VII from 1685, until he was deposed on 11 December 1688. Son of Dunfermline-born Charles I and brother of Charles II, James was in Scotland in 1679 and 1680, and Elie tradition has it that he lodged at the house of one Alexander Gillespie, called the 'Muckle Yett'; this house is long demolished, but its 'yett' (doorway) is to be seen at the Gillespie House (rebuilt 1870) in South Street.

James' presence gave rise to a village tale. It seems that during one visit the coxswain of the royal duke's barge fell for a local girl. Her family opposed the match, but the pair were married in secret by the minister of Kilconquhar. After the nuptials the new bride was smuggled aboard the royal barge in a fish barrel. As the barrel was being hoisted on to the barge, with great care, an onlooker enquired why such care was being taken. The reply was that a swan from Kilconquhar Loch was being taken to Holyrood Palace. The story was recounted in a ballad, which served as a warning to Elie lasses:

> They stowed the maiden in a cask
> And bore her to the shore;
> And it's fare-ye-weel my father's house
> And Elie evermore.

Sing a' and sing a': sing, Elie laddies a',
Bewaur the Duke o'York's lads
When they come here awa'.

FALKLAND

The small town of Falkland, in a parish once known as Kilgour and at the foot of the East Lomond, developed from a castle-dominated village; its own green was long known as 'the frequent scene of dancing and revelry'. The great central tower of the castle stood a short distance to the north of the present Falkland Palace layout, and portions of extant stone on site suggest that the castle existed from at least the thirteenth century. It was the home and fortress of the MacDuffs, earls of Fife, within a burgh of barony; the MacDuffs were important hereditary courtiers of the Scottish court and significant role players in the realm's early medieval history. By 1371 the MacDuff heiress, Isabel, Countess of Fife, resigned the earldom to her brother-in-law Robert Stewart, Earl of Mentieth, brother of Robert III. In this way the castle, its dependent village and rich forest land became Stewart properties and thence Crown domain.

Down the brutal historical sequence of Scottish political jockeying, the castle of Falkland came into the ownership of James II 'of the Fiery Face' (r.1437–60), who changed its description from castle to palace. By now the village of Falkland had developed into a little town and James granted it the honorary status of royal burgh in 1458. The charter was renewed by James VI in 1595, which preserved the local markets and fairs.

James II began to develop a new palace but little of this remains as it was burned down by Cromwell's Ironsides in 1645. When James IV succeeded to the throne in 1488 he continued building work, added to by his son James V to make the palace one of the United Kingdom's finest architectural treasures. When James V died in 1542 work on the palace ceased, but it remained a royal possession.

Once Falkland thrived as an important part of the royal infrastructure; in the village, then town, lived courtiers and royal servants and a myriad of staff. Some of their dwellings are still to be seen in such buildings as Moncrieff House (1610) in High Street. Many of these houses were restored by the National Trust for Scotland in the 'Little Houses' scheme.

The three great offices of the palace, the Captain, the Constable and the Keeper (quite often the same person) gave steady employment to Falkland folk and certain families became hereditary Keepers of this and that. In 1887 one such Keeper of the Palace, John Crichton Stuart, 3rd Marquess of Bute, began a huge restoration programme for the palace and gardens and in 1952 the Crichton Stuarts handed the palace to the keeping of the National Trust for Scotland. Today the palace, with its Chapel Royal, gardens and Royal Tennis Court, is the centrepiece of Falkland.

Falkland developed around the East and West Port, High Street and a web of wynds, and its Scottish Court associations resulted in it becoming the first designated Conservation Area in Scotland. A Town Hall was built in the High Street during 1800–01, to be bought by the National Trust for Scotland in 1986; here is housed a display on the history of Falkland. The Victorian Gothic parish church stands on the site of a 1620 church and was constructed during 1849–50, opposite the 1856 fountain on the site of the medieval mercat cross; both the latter were the gift of a former Keeper of the Palace, one Onesiphorus Tyndall-Bruce, who also built the House of Falkland, a Jacobean mansion of 1839–44. Bruce's statue is to be found next to the parish church.

When the patronage of the Scottish court waned, after the Union of the Crowns in 1603, Falkland developed as a town of handloom weavers.

Falkland grew to national fame because of its royal connections, but not every burgher in the town's highways and byways was pro-royal. At the south-west corner of The Cross area stands the once-thatched Cameron House, a seventeenth-century edifice remembering one such anti-monarchist. Here in 1648 was born Richard Cameron, the son of a small general dealer at Falkland. He first appears in recorded history as a schoolmaster and precentor (a person who leads or directs a choir/congregation). Cameron was converted from episcopacy to presbyterianism by 'field preachers' and became preceptor (tutor) to the family of Sir Walter Scott of Harden. He was soon removed from that position through his confrontation with the local parish minister. Thereafter Cameron became a licensed preacher, often at odds with superiors in the kirk. In 1678 he sought spiritual exile in Holland, returning in 1680. He then became leader of a militant group of 'reformed Presbyterians' popularly known as the 'Cameronians' and on 20 June 1680, at Sanquhar, Dumfriesshire, renounced all allegiance to Charles II,

Falkland, the favourite palace of several Stewart monarchs; Mary, Queen of Scots hunted its forests and the royal court helped to develop the surrounding village which received royal charter in 1458. The tower of the Old Town House is seen to the left. [*Author's collection*]

declaring war against him and opposition to Charles's named successor, his Roman Catholic brother James, Duke of York. Cameron was now a marked man with a price of 5,000 merks on his head set by the Privy Council. On 20 July 1680 Cameron and his band were discovered at Aird's Moss, Ayrshire, by a royalist military band under Fifer Bruce of Earlshall. Cameron was slain in the resultant skirmish, his head and hands being severed as trophies to be affixed to the Netherbow Port at Edinburgh. Charles II was the last royal resident ever to grace Falkland Palace.

FERNIE

Once within the estates of the earls of Fife, the lands were divided into Easter and Wester Fernie, with Easter Fernie being the predominant hamlet. The family of Fernie were once the hereditary Foresters of Falkland and Constables of Cupar Castle. The House of Fernie (formerly Fairnie) was a substantial sixteenth-century fortress which developed into modern Fernie Castle and is now a hotel.

Cunnoquhie was once a part of the estate of Fernie; here an eighteenth-century house developed into a late nineteenth-century mansion.

FERRY-PORT-ON-CRAIG (see: TAYPORT)

FOODIEASH

Once part of the estate of Foodie, at the beginning of the seventeenth century the estate was in the hands of Sir James Hay of Kingask, whose son, another Sir James, was a courtier and favourite of James VI. This Sir James travelled to England with James VI in 1603 and later became the king's ambassador to France; he was elevated to the viscountcy of Doncaster (Yorkshire) in 1618; further diplomatic missions were rewarded with the earldom of Carlisle and titles Keeper of the Great Wardrobe and Groom of the Stole. Charles I granted him the island of Barbados. Foodie estate was subsequently sold to the Wemysses of Wemyss and thence to the Earl of Elgin, to pass down to proprietors who developed its agricultural potential. The village was thus a farming community set by an old road which linked Falkland and Dairsie in medieval times. Foodieash village school is now a private house.

FREUCHIE

The village has long been immortalised in historical clichés. When James V was embellishing Falkland Palace there were French artists among his craftsmen. It is believed that they were quartered at Freuchie. In the memories of the old folk of Freuchie were these dismissive phrases: 'Awa tae Freuchie whaur the Froggies bide', and 'Awa tae Freuchie and eat frogs'.

By the eighteenth century Freuchie had evolved as a village of handloom weavers, the industry expanding with the construction of Lumsden's Linen Mill at Eden Valley Road around 1870. Once Freuchie village was known for the manufacture of window-blinds. A parish church was built in the High Street in 1876 as well as Lumsden Memorial Hall in 1883. Freuchie Corn Mill dates from 1840. A variety of eighteenth- and nineteenth-century buildings remain while the Lomond Hills Hotel dates from 1753.

FORDELL

A former mining village in old Dalgety parish. To the south of the village, in a wooded park on the edge of a ravine above the Keithing Burn, lies the 1567–80 tower-house of Fordell Castle built for the Hendersons, who acquired the lands of Fordell in 1511. The castle has its own detached chapel of 1650 with a vaulted crypt of around 1855. The whole is based on a thirteenth-century estate – St Thereota's Lands – gifted to the abbey of Inchcolm by Richard de Camera around 1220. The Hendersons invested heavily in the local coal and salt industries. Across the estate once ran Scotland's first private railway, transporting coal to St David's harbour.

GALLATOWN

Formerly Easter and Wester Gallowtown. Local historians dispute its name; some aver it comes from *geal* (white), while others such as the Rev. John Campbell of Kirkcaldy Parish Church said (1924): '[the village] was the place where justice was carried out by the lord of the Manor'. The village core probably dates from the late seventeenth century, within the ownership of the Earl of Rosslyn, but most older dwellings are of the nineteenth century. Again this was a place of nail manufacture (seventeenth century), coalmining and power-loom weaving (mid-eighteenth century) and pottery manufacture (from 1817), and became absorbed into modern Kirkcaldy.

GATESIDE

Once this village was dubbed 'The Chapeltown of the Virgin' (*Capellaniae Sanctae Mariae de Dungaitsyd*), because it owed its foundation to the presence of a chapel dedicated to the Blessed Virgin within the barony of Pitgarno, and was a dependency of the abbey of Balmerino. These properties were gifted to the abbey of Balmerino by Princess Marjorie, Countess of Pembroke and daughter of William the Lion, around 1240. Today its heart is a small vernacular village of eighteenth- and nineteenth-century houses, with Gateside Mill to the south-east by the River Eden. Gateside, formerly Edenshead, was once known for its linen manufacture and its bobbin and shuttle mills. Disused Gateside church dates from 1823 and a primary school from 1875.

GAULDRY

Now largely a dormitory village, 'The Gauldry', as it is known, was once a weaving community. Its parish church dates from 1867 and is the site of the school for the parish of Balmerino.

GLENBURNIE

Village within the parish of Abdie and the early medieval lands of the earls of Fife. Once known for its sawmills.

GLENCRAIG

On the estate of Glencraig and within the old parish of Ballingry, a hamlet was established here after 1840, a neighbour of the cluster of mining settlements hereabouts.

GLENDUCKIE

This village lies within, and is the only settlement in, the parish of Flisk; the parish has no eponymous village, only a church, a manse and neighbouring farms. The mid nineteenth-century farmhouse of Balhelvie has a round horse mill of note, while Fliskmillan sports buildings of Georgian and mid-Victorian date. Flisk Parish Church (1790) is now a roofless shell with graveyard, while its manse (Wester Flisk) dates from 1811; additions to church and manse were made in 1886.

The pre-Reformation church of Flisk has now vanished, but records show that it was rededicated in September 1242 by David de Bernham, Bishop of St Andrews, to St Adrian and St Macgriden.

Glenduckie, at the foot of Glenduckie Hill, was once within the estates of the earls of Fife, but by the time the earls of Rothes held the barony of Ballinbreich (first formed in 1312), the village was within that barony. By 1601 Glenduckie was united with the newly created barony of Aytoun. The village once had its own chapel, still extant in 1682, and corn mill, both supplying rents to the Leslies. Glenduckie Hill has a presumed Iron Age homestead.

A neighbour of Glenduckie is the ruined castle of Ballinbreich (pronounced Balmbreich), which in its earliest form dates from the fourteenth century, habitation of the Leslies, earls of Rothes. The castle was reconstructed around 1572 for Alexander Leslie, Earl of Rothes, and contained its own fourteenth-century chapel.

GLENROTHES

From 1948 the Glenrothes Development Corporation was responsible for the foundation of the new town. The first houses and schools were begun in 1951, the first shops in 1952, and the first church, St Margaret's Parish Church, in 1954. Historically Glenrothes is set out on land from the old Rothes, Balfour, Balgonie and Aytoun estates. The development area only had two villages, Cadham and Woodside.

Cadham

The Earl of Rothes opened a colliery here in 1741. Modern mining area developed 1851–81. Name retained in housing estate.

Woodside

Location of first Glenrothes Development Corporation constructions by 1950. Name retained in housing estate.

GOWKHALL

Weaving village, parish of Carnock, established with a few houses by the 1790s.

GRANGE OF LINDORES

This is an old monastic site for the Tironesian Abbey of St Mary and St Andrew at Lindores had a granary here. When the abbey was secularised at the Reformation, Grange of Lindores, with other abbey farms at Ormiston, Berryhill and Hilton, fell to lay owners. The Priest's Burn, from Lindores Loch to the Tay, once supplied power for nine corn mills. Today Grange of Lindores presents itself as an early nineteenth-century rural hamlet with a mid nineteenth-century school.

GUARDBRIDGE

The village of Guardbridge had an important place in Fife's maritime medieval history long before the start of the William Haig Seggie Distillery of around 1810 and the paper industry (1872). The Moonzie

Guardbridge paper mill complex was developed from an old distillery, from 1872, where the Motray Water meets the River Eden. This aerial picture of the late 1940s shows the area once the medieval harbour for St Andrews. The mill promoted and supported the village of Guardbridge. [*Mrs Hilda Kirkwood*]

Burn and the Motray Water join the River Eden to the north of Guardbridge and here the early village began. In 1381 Robert II granted a charter to the burgesses of Cupar to 'possess a free port in the water of Motray'. Even then the local quays were old for in 1209 King John of England allowed Seyer de Quincy, Earl of Winchester, to send one of his Guardbridge-based vessels into English waters. The village developed as a homebase for the paper mill workforce between 1887 and the late 1930s.

Guardbridge had two bridges of note, the Inner Bridge, over the Motray Water, a probable sixteenth-century structure with an early eighteenth-century makeover, and the six-arched Guard Bridge over the Eden. The latter was built by Henry Wardlaw, Bishop of St Andrews (1404–40), and was then mentioned in documents as *Le gare-brig*; *gare-gair* means a triangular portion of land. Repair work was done on the orders of Archbishop James Beaton (1522–39), whose arms and initials appear on panels on either side of the bridge. A modern bridge was built alongside in 1939 and the piers of the old railway bridge to St Andrews (line closed in 1969) are still to be seen. In this area was a gathering place for medieval pilgrims so that they could journey to St Andrews Cathedral under guard through the wild places of Kincaple.

HALBEATH

A small mining village that is now almost totally merged with Dunfermline. Once a horse railway operated between Halbeath and Inverkeithing; opened in 1783 for the transportation of coal, this wagon-road lasted until 1867. Here is sited Lauder College of 1964, extended in 1976. In the grounds is early Victorian Fod House.

HATTON LAW

A rural hamlet associated in history with Pitcruivie Castle, a late fifteenth-century edifice overlooking the Keil Burn. The fourteenth-century estate came into the ownership of the Lindsays in 1498 and the castle fell into disuse following the tenancy of James Watson, Provost of St Andrews, in the seventeenth century.

HILL END

Rural hamlet at the foot of Welter Hill.

HILLEND

A hamlet at the foot of Letham Hill Wood. Now being encroached on by the western development of Dalgety Bay.

HILL OF BEATH

Old mining hamlet by the Hill of Beath.

HOLEKETTLE (see: KETTLEBRIDGE)

HOSPITAL MILL (see: CULTS)

INNERLEVEN

Area by the harbours of Leven at the mouth of the River Leven, a development of the amalgam of the Buckhaven–Methil–Leven sprawl. From here fish was sent to the medieval clergy at St Drostan's, Markinch. The settlement appears at various times as Coldcoits, Dubbieside and Salt-grieve.

INVERKEITHING

Inverkeithing first enters recorded history in a charter granted to the Augustinian abbey at Scone of 1114–15, and it is mentioned again as a burgh in the days of Malcolm IV (1153–65). Its earliest surviving charter dates from 1178–89 and tradition has it that William the Lion elevated it to royal burgh status as one of the first acts of his reign from 1165. Today the historic core of Inverkeithing lies west of the railway line. From the early twelfth century the predominant family was that of Gospatrick, Earl of Dunbar, but in time influence passed to the Moubrays of Barnbougle who retained prominence until the seventeenth century.

Records show that David I set the fashion for Inverkeithing as a medieval watering place. Robert III's wife, Annabella Drummond, resided at Rotmills Inns in the town and died there in 1403. So important was the town that the Convention of Royal Burghs was held here in 1487 and the town's royal status was confirmed by James VI in 1598. Inverkeithing's quays on the Forth were ideal for a flourishing trade, already established by 1129 when they were in the care of the abbots of Dunfermline. A village developed in what is now High Street, Bank Street, Townhall Street and Church Street. Once Inverkeithing had walls and four ports (gates) which were removed in the sixteenth century.

While the streets offer a variety of seventeenth–nineteenth-century buildings, from Fordell's Lodging (*c.*1670) to the sixteenth-century Rosebery House, a number of key sites are important in plotting Inverkeithing's development from village to town.

In Church Street stands the parish church of St Peter, thought to have started as a wooden Celtic church that developed into a Norman stone structure bequeathed to Dunfermline Abbey in 1139. All that remains of the pre-Reformation church of 1480 is the tower; the church was destroyed by fire in 1825. It was rebuilt in 1826 and restored in 1900. During excavations in 1807 a font was discovered – probably hidden from the Reformer despoilers – which is thought to have been a gift of Annabella Drummond and Robert III at the baptism of their son, David, Duke of Rothesay.

The Hospitium of Greyfriars Monastery stands in Queen Street and was possibly founded as early as the thirteenth century by Philip de Moubray, Lord of Barnbougle, and was used by friars of the Order of St Francis. The friary was restored in 1932–4. Inverkeithing's townhouse with its pepperpot steeple replaced an older (before 1550) tolbooth in 1770. Above the door of the townhouse is the old burgh's coat of arms; it shows St Peter the Apostle and Martyr. There is a tiara, key and a church on the dexter side of the arms, and a ship and a church on the sinister side. Inverkeithing's mercat cross has had a number of sites. Originally it stood at the north end of High Street and was moved to face the townhouse in 1799; today it is located in Bank Street. Like most medieval burghs Inverkeithing had four annual fairs and it is known that James IV bought his horses at the Lammas Fair (August).

By the mid-1700s Inverkeithing had declined, but a late eighteenth-century ironworks and distillery revived fortunes. Inverkeithing became known for its shipbuilding, shipbreaking and its paper mill. Today Inverkeithing is largely a commuter town for Edinburgh.

Excavations during the 1980s in the High Street area confirmed its prosperous medieval past; the exposed cobbled surfaces showed much traffic of carts and sleds making their way to and from the Keithing Burn. Pottery finds revealed imports from such places as Germany, Holland and France being used by the locals. Animal bones were discovered too, showing Inverkeithing's taste for horsemeat.

Inverkeithing

As befits a settlement with important maritime connections, Inverkeithing had a local hero in Sir Samuel Greig. Born at Inverkeithing in 1735, Greig's family ran the *Thistle*, a small vessel which traded with Russia. From an apprenticeship in the Merchant Navy, Greig passed into the Royal Navy and served there until 1763. He was present at the Battle of Quiberon Bay, a peninsula in north-west France on the south coast of Brittany, where in 1759 during the Seven Years' War the Royal Navy defeated the French fleet. By 1764 Greig had entered the service of the Russian Imperial Navy of Catherine the Great, and commanded a division under Admiral Orloff at Chesme Bay in 1770 during the war with the Turks. He was appointed Rear-Admiral in 1770, Vice-Admiral in 1773, then Grand Admiral and Governor of Kronstadt, where he designed the fortifications. He commanded the Russian Navy against Sweden in action at Hogland in 1788 during the Baltic War of 1788–90. Greig was hailed as 'Father of the Russian Navy', staffing it largely with

Scottish officers. His son Admiral Alexis Samuelovich Greig (1775–1845) carried on the family tradition.

JAMESTOWN

This area lies at the northern edge of the Ferry Hills by the inner bay of Inverkeithing Bay. Once magnesia was worked here and salt panned, but the whole was better known for the nearby shipbreaking yards. Jamestown takes its name from James Reid who converted the old chemical works into dwellings.

KELTY

Set abutting the border of Fife and Perthshire and flanked by Blairadam Forest to the west, Kelty developed as a substantial mining village from the 1880s. Within the old parish of Beath, its oldest buildings, three churches and primary school all date from the mid-1890s. It was at Kelty that the Fife Coal Co. was developed from 1872, to take in the main acquisitions of Hill of Beath (1887); Cowdenbeath (1896); Lochore and Capledrae (1900); Blairadam (1901); and Bowhill (1909). The collieries, lands and properties were nationalised in 1946, but the works are now defunct. In medieval times the area was described as Keltywood and Keltyheuch and were lands conferred by James VI during 1593–4 on his queen, Anne of Denmark. From the early 1600s coal was mined at Keltyheuch by William, Earl of Morton.

KEMBACK

This scattered community, spread along the Ceres Burn before it joins the Eden Water near Dairsie Castle, is associated in history with the spinning community of Dura Den and Milton of Blebo. Kemback had its nineteenth-century meal, bone and saw mills, while nearby Nydie Mill was for meal. Today it incorporates dwellings at Kemback Bridge and nineteenth-century Yoolbank Crescent. The Schevez family obtained the estate of Kemback and in 1478 supplied an archbishop of St Andrews in William Schevez.

Kemback's old roofless parish church was built in 1582 as a rectory of the archbishopric of St Andrews and as a gift to the College of St Salvator; enlarged in 1760 it was preserved in 1960. A newer parish church dates from 1810–14, its manse to 1801, while a former manse (thatched to 1758) is probably seventeenth century.

Kemback House is an early eighteenth-century building given 'baronial treatment' in 1907. Described by Sir James Sibbald in 1803 as 'a sweet place, well planted', he went on to associate it with one Myles Graham, one of the murderers of James I, who forfeited the property in 1437 when it reverted to the archbishopric of St Andrews. The most prominent family associated with the estate were the Mackgills, of the same family as that of Rankeillour who held prestigious positions at the Stewart court.

KENNOWAY

In medieval times the land around here had religious and secular owners, the first in the Augustinian priors of St Andrews and the second in the earls of Rothes. A not unusual example in Fife history of lands and a village which were the personal property of a family, Kennoway's early village activities were oat and barley mills, flax processing and spinning. Prosperity was further founded in the malting and brewing industry until the mid-1750s when this failed and the village declined. By the late 1700s weaving had been introduced; this prospered until the later nineteenth century.

Most of Kennoway's early village buildings were made from sandstone quarried at Kennoway Den. A Burgher chapel dates from the 1700s period of prosperity and was made into the Arnot Gospel Hall of 1870–75. A parish church here with associated lands, dedicated to St Kenneth, once belonged to the Augustinian priory of St Andrews, but a new building was constructed 1849–50.

The old main street of Kennoway is retained in the Causeway. This was the focal point of the developing village and was once on the turnpike route between the ferries of Pettycur and Tayport; the rerouting of this highway via New Inn was a contributory factor to Kennoway's first main decline. Forbes House (*c.* 1800) and Seton House (eighteenth century) both claim to have sheltered Archbishop James Sharp on his last night before his murder at Magus Muir in 1679. Kennoway remains a dormitory habitation which saw modern expansion with the coming of Ayrshire miners in 1930 and 1950. Just to the south of Kennoway at Dunipace lie the remains of a motte known as Maiden Castle and associated in local legend with Macduff, Earl of Fife.

KETTLEBRIDGE

Kettlebridge is an early nineteenth-century development along the A92 Cupar to Glenrothes road. It began as a hamlet for linen weavers and forms a triangle of mid- and late nineteenth-century habitations between the A92 and the 1847 railway embankment. Near Kettlebridge once stood Brankton House, the long vanished home of James Russell, one of the murderers of Archbishop James Sharp in 1679.

KETTLEHILL

A hamlet in the old coal and quarry area adjacent to Kingskettle. In medieval times the lands were held by Duncan, Earl of Fife, as a grant from Malcolm IV in 1166. Today it forms part of an agricultural and dormitory area.

KILCONQUHAR

The village, pronounced 'Kinucher', stands on the shores of an eponymous loch which seems to have taken form before 1599. Set on a knoll by the shores of the loch, the parish church was built in 1819–21, its 80-ft tower a distinctive landmark. The former manse dates from 1814–15. There was a church here as early as the twelfth century that was in the care of the nuns of North Berwick at Ardross. The area was once an important source of fuel (peat) and turf for the village and the ecclesiastical grange. Opposite the church stands the early eighteenth-century Kinneuchar Inn. The village offers a range of eighteenth- and nineteenth-century houses, with much renovation, and a war memorial stands in a small square area instead of a mercat cross.

To the east of the village lies Kilconquhar Castle and the remains of an earlier castle. The original castle was built in 1547 on the lands of Sir John Bellenden, Lord Justice-Clerk in the reign of James V. It then passed to Sir John Carstairs in 1634, and until recent times was the 1831–9 seat of the earls of Lindsay. The castle was badly damaged by fire in 1978, but has been restored as the centrepiece of an estate of multi-ownership holiday villas.

KILMANY

A leafy hamlet by the Motray Water, the village forms an area of new housing developments and refurbished old properties. Anciently the church belonging to the episcopate of St Andrews, it subsequently became a gift to the College of St Salvator by Bishop James Kennedy.

A former rector of Kilmany was James Bruce who became Bishop of Dunkeld in 1441 and Lord Chancellor of Scotland. The present church dates from 1768 and the surrounding graveyard has a selection of noteworthy eighteenth-century table stones of fine workmanship. Historians have noted that buried in the churchyard is the Earl of Melville, one of the Scottish noblemen who supported William of Orange when he became joint ruler with Mary II in 1689. Kilmany Manse dates from 1809–10 and here dwelt Dr Thomas Chalmers (1780–1847), one of the most distinguished pulpit and lecture-hall orators of his day; he held the professorships of Moral Philosophy at St Andrews (1823) and of Divinity (1828) at Edinburgh and became the first Moderator of the General Assembly of the Free Church.

Kilmany House, 1914–19, incorporates an earlier dwelling of 1816. By the Motray Water stands a statue to the memory of racing driver Jim Clark (1936–68), born at Kilmany and killed in a motor race at Hokenheim.

KILRENNY

Once referred to as Upper Kilrenny (cf. Nether Kilrenny, or Cellardyke) the village owes its historical character to weaving, fishing and agriculture. Today its street names offer clues as to the structure of the medieval village: Kirk Wynd leads to the village's commercial heart of Trade Street which once rang to the hammers of the farriers and shoemakers. Most folk hereabouts worked on the land or at the fishing and lived in cottar houses such as those developed in Routine Row. These days the village, now bypassed by the A917, offers a range of modified eighteenth- and nineteenth-century dwellings with a schoolhouse of 1840 and a school (now a village hall) of 1815.

Tradition has it that in 864 a chapel was erected at Kilrenny dedicated to St Ethernan, a companion of St Adrian of May Island. Around 1177 the lands and privileges of Kilrethni were given by Ada de Warenne, wife of Prince Henry, Earl of Northumberland, and thereby daughter-in-law of David I, to the chapter of Dryburgh Abbey, Berwickshire; the monks jealously guarded their fishing rights over which they were often in dispute with the clergy on May Island. The Premonstratensians of Dryburgh sponsored a church on the site of an earlier edifice and it was rededicated in 1243. The church was demolished in 1807–08 when the present one replaced it; the fifteenth-century tower, once used as a landmark by fishing skippers, is all that remains of an earlier building. The church was renovated in 1933 and retains its plain interior, but with a fine reredos; a crow-stepped Romanesque porch dates from 1932.

Near to the foot of the church tower is the huge 1832 tomb of the Lumisdaines of Innergellie. A near neighbour is the massive mausoleum erected *c.*1776 by the Duchess of Portland in memory of her father, General Scot of Balcomie. Local legend has it that when the Protestant mob prepared to attack the Dominican chapel of the Blackfriars at St Andrews in 1559, relatives of Cardinal David Beaton, Archbishop of St Andrews, who had been murdered at his castle-palace at St Andrews in 1546, moved his despised bones from the chapel and hid them at Kilrenny church. The Beaton burial enclosure dates from the late seventeenth century.

By the reign of James III, 1437–60, the lands of Kilrenny seem to have fallen to the Crown which conferred them on the Beatons of Balfour whose mansion at Kilrenny has now disappeared. In 1578 John Beaton of Balfour was given a charter electing Kilrenny into the status of burgh of regality by Patrick Adamson, titular Archbishop of St Andrews. This also allowed a market cross to be erected and for the villagers to hold a weekly Sabbath market and two annual fairs on 30 April and 25 October. Kilrenny once had political importance, sponsoring its own MP in the Scottish Parliament between 1612–1707.

Innergellie house at Kilrenny sits on lands which were once part of the marriage dowry of Annabella Drummond, wife of Robert III (r.1390–1406) and were long the properties of the de Spaldings. Subsequently owned by the Barclays of Kippo, the property was purchased by Sir James Lumisdaine of Airdrie estate. The present baroque mansion dates from 1740 and has a statue of Hermes (Mercurius to the Romans) high above the pediment with a coat of arms of 1630 and an octagonal tower. Near by is a lectern doocot. The house became the home of the Sandys-Lumisdaines from 1830 and the family occupied the house until the 1960s.

Recent interest in Fife's Pictish past has focused interest on the Kilrenny Stone. Kilrenny village site was, from around 297, within the tribal lands of the warrior Venicones. In 1993 a fragment of Pictish symbol stone was found on the nearby beach which may well have been carved and erected by Venicones tribesfolk. A further fragment of the same stone was found at Cornceres Farm in 1997. Experts have stated that the matching fragments are part of a ninth-century cross-slab bearing a Celtic cross and a type of mythical vulpine beast. The slab was probably shattered at the Reformation for reuse as building materials.

KINCAPLE

A small hamlet in the old parish of St Andrews in lands which before the Reformation were within the acres of the Augustinian priory of St Andrews. In medieval times it was a wild land of scrub, forest and marsh, the haunt of outlaws who used to prey on unguarded pilgrims heading for the shrine of St Andrew. In 1587 Kincaple lands passed to the Crown and were partially gifted to James Melville, Constable of St Andrews Castle, for his diplomatic services to the Danish court. From the seventeenth century the properties of Kincaple were divided among various succeeding heritors.

In the late 1700s the hamlet supported a distillery which John Leighton described in 1840 as 'extensive'. The brewery was transferred to Seggie (in modern Guardbridge), in Leuchars parish, but in the mid-1800s the malt barns were still in use. Here too inhabitants were employed in a now vanished brickworks and the papermill at Guardbridge.

Kincaple House is an interesting laird's house of 1789, now divided into separate dwellings with others in its grounds. It began life as Bloomfield Farm and wings were added in 1927.

KINCARDINE-ON-FORTH

Note: Before 1891 Tulliallan and Kincardine were a detached portion of Perthshire. Kincardine was an ancient crossing area of the Forth, with an established ferry into the twentieth century to Higgins' Neuk, Stirlingshire. Ferry services were discontinued after the opening of the 2,696-ft swing bridge across the Forth in 1936. (The bridge was permanently fixed in 1988.)

The settlement that would grow into Kincardine-on-Forth was

made a burgh of barony in 1663, and constructed on reclaimed marshland when the Fife coastal region was infilled with deposits of coal ash from the salt-panning industry; from this activity Kincardine had once been called West Pans. Nevertheless a now vanished hamlet was probably set out in the vicinity of the old castle, with a thoroughfare to the medieval ferry. In time Kincardine evolved as a prime port and developed shipyards; salt, papermaking and quarry products were transported from here by water. Kincardine's old harbour area is still to be seen although its oldest part is traversed by the road bridge of 1932–6; it consists of the Shipping Pier (1811–13); the Viscount Keith West Embankment (1823, 1836 and 1891); the Ferry Pier (1826); and the East Embankment (1829–38).

Kincardine has two castles called Tulliallan. By Devilla Forest, Tulliallan was once a wild area, the sanctuary of outlaws and ne'er-do-wells. At Kirk Brae is the Tulliallan Castle Scottish Police College (1954) set within the 1817–19 home of Admiral Viscount Keith who bought the estate in 1798.

At Castlepark lies a ruined early fourteenth-century building, convenient to a medieval ferry across the Forth. It is said that at one time the Forth washed the walls of this Tulliallan Castle. It won some prominence in Scottish history by being the home of the Blackadders. One important member of this family was Robert Blackadder, Bishop of Glasgow 1483–1508, in whose episcopate Glasgow became a metropolitan church. This castle of Tulliallan was probably already a strong fortress when Edward I invaded Scotland and had the castle strengthened in 1304 as an important strategic position on the Forth. The castle was probably abandoned as a home by the seventeenth century.

Kincardine also has two parish churches. The Old is set at Wood Lea, and is a roofless ruin within a graveyard and dates from 1675–6. The old graveyard reflects the seafaring nature of the ancient community with its symbols of death interspersed with ships in sail. The New kirk in Kirk Street dates from 1832–3 with a landmark tower. A seventeenth-century mercat cross is sited in High Street. A variety of eighteenth- and nineteenth-century houses can be seen.

KINGHORN

Kinghorn was already an ancient settlement when David I created it a royal burgh in the twelfth century. Kinghorn's castle, once referred

Alexander III Memorial

to as Glamis Tower, because of its ownership by the Lyons of Glamis, has now vanished, but was once a favourite haven for both monarchs and nobles alike. A jointure of Scotland's queens, it was to Kinghorn Castle that Alexander III, the last of Scotland's Celtic kings, was making his way on the stormy night of 19 March 1286, when he came to grief over the precipice of Kinghorn Ness.

After a decline in the early 1700s, Kinghorn saw a flurry of rebuilding from the 1800s to develop as an important ferryport. Before its townhouse was built in 1826, the site was occupied by a medieval edifice, St Leonard's Tower; the latter has been identified, on somewhat shaky premises, as a chapel belonging to the Dominican preaching friars in 1388. The 1774 parish church stands by the sea, down Nethergate, and is on the site of several churches from Saxon times. The present one was rebuilt in 1894–5 and internally reconstructed in 1930; outside is the ruined choir of an earlier church,

Kinghorn became a royal burgh in 1170 with an important medieval fortified royal dwelling. Its village core prospered as a ferry port for the Forth. Kinghorn parish church of 1774 is seen on the right by eighteenth-century Kirk Harbour. [*Author's collection*]

probably the one rededicated by Bishop David de Bernham of St Andrews in 1243. In medieval times Kinghorn had a hospital for the poor founded around 1478 and set within the grounds of a chapel dedicated to St James.

Because of its royal court connections, several neighbouring estates have featured in Kinghorn's history. Piteadie Castle was once the home of the Earl of Rosslyn and Sir Henry Wardlaw (d.1631), chamberlain to James VI's queen, Anne of Denmark. The Wardlaws also owned the property at Abden, where Sir John Melville had a mansion house of 1542 on land once beloning to the Archbishop of St Andrews; Melville was executed for high treason in 1549. Offering a range of interesting eighteenth- and nineteenth-century dwellings, Kinghorn today serves as a dormitory area for Edinburgh and Kirkcaldy.

Out of medieval Kinghorn came John of Kinghorn, who, in the reign of James V (1513–42) became court surgeon to the Danish King Christian III of the Oldenburg dynasty. He is one of the early Fife medics to be known by name. Incidentally several nationally known doctors had Fife connections. Sir Robert Sibbald (1641–1722) of Gibliston, near Arncroach, is one example. Sibbald became President of the Edinburgh Royal College of Physicians and was physician to Charles II. With another Fife medic, Sir Andrew Balfour (1630–94) of Denmylne, near Newburgh, he co-founded Edinburgh's Botanical Gardens. To this roster can be added the surgeon James Syme (1799–1870) and John Goodsir (1814–67) the anatomist and Professor of Anatomy at Edinburgh University. Goodsir came from a prominent Anstruther medical family celebrated in a local poem, said to have been written by Lady Anne Lindsay (see: 'Auld Robin Gray') and published in *The Bee* in 1792:

> If spleen oppress thy soul, or bod'ly pain
> Racks every joint, and cramps thy ev'ry vein,
> Here breathe the air which will thy health restore,
> Cheer all thy soul, and open ev'ry pore;
> Or if by slow consumption you decay,
> Come here and live – there's life in Largo Bay;
> Bathe in the stream which braces every nerve,
> Goodsir declares this will thy life preserve.
> And who can doubt what Goodsir doth declare,
> Whose medicines are always mixed with prayer.

KINGLASSIE

This old roadside weaving village – once called Goatmilk – gave its later name to the surrounding agricultural parish. In history the lands hereabouts were 'mortified' by charitable bequest in 1122 to the Benedictine Abbey of Dunfermline, by Queen Sibylla, natural daughter of Henry I of England and wife of Alexander I; thereafter the monks feued the acres to various parties until they became Crown properties again and were later purchased by John, Duke of Rothes, and later still acquired by the Balfours of Balbirnie. Founded around 1800, probably from an extant hamlet, Kinglassie's village character was changed with the opening of the Kinglassie Colliery around 1900.

Kinglassie had a medieval church, and its present parish church dates from 1773–4 and 1887–8, with an interior revamped 1890–91. A manse was built in 1774 and repaired in 1818, and a parish school dates from 1796–7. A primary school evolved in 1912. The associated mining infrastructure of buildings and huge bings have now gone.

To the north of the village, on Redwell's Hill, stands the tower known as 'Blythe's Folly'; this 52-ft tower was built in 1812 by an eccentric Leith shipowner. At Whinnyhall, to the left of the B921 as it enters the village, is the site of an invader's fort, and in the marsh a Roman sword was found in 1830. Just south of Kinglassie, by Pitlochie, stands the Dogton Cross, an ancient Celtic monument with traces of animal and figure sculpture.

KINGSBARNS

The site of the recently constructed Kingsbarns Golf Course allowed archaeologists to add vital information to what is known about Kingsbarns village. Local legend has it that Kingsbarns Castle, which has now vanished but was situated between the east end of the village and the sea, was a favourite residence of King John Baliol (r.1292–6). Nearby were sited grain stores for the harvest of the surrounding Crown lands; the accumulated bulk grain was transported to Falkland Castle. In the eighteenth century, local tradition has it, a tenant farmer removed stones from the castle site to make a harbour wall. The castle gave rise to a dependent hamlet.

Recent excavation has proved Bronze Age and Iron Age activity, located a bridge and reidentified that the village supported a nine-hole golf course of 1815 set out by the Kingsbarns Golfing Society, which had been founded in 1793.

Kingsbarns remains the only village in its eponymous parish, disjoined from Crail in 1631. The village had two cattle fairs in July and October, which later dwindled to a hucksters' fair in the early nineteenth century. A church was erected at Kingsbarns in 1631 to be enlarged in 1810–11, and a manse was built 1834–5. The community developed as a weaving and agricultural village with a primary school of 1822. Kingsbarns retains the form of a village square with pump (1831). The village offers an interesting collection of eighteenth-century housing and Cambo Arms Hotel is a Georgian coaching inn.

Just to the south of Kingsbarns lies Cambo estate, which, records show, was given to one Robert de Newenham around 1250 by William the Lion; de Newenham's descendants assumed the name de Cambhou. Thereafter it belonged to the Myretons (Mortons), who sold it through Sir Thomas Morton in 1688 to Sir Charles Erskine, Lyon King at Arms, brother of the Earl of Kellie; the Erskines still own the estate. The estate survived in its medieval form until it was given a 'designer landscape' in the seventeenth century and revamped in the eighteenth century. In 1878 the old mansion house was

Pitmilly House

destroyed by fire to be replaced by the extant mansion of 1879–81.

Kingsbarns has a number of neighbours worthy of note. Randerston House is a late sixteenth-century edifice and Wormiston dates from the seventeenth century. Pitmilly estate was held by the Monypennys for six centuries from the time that Richardus de Monypenny obtained the land from Thomas, Prior of St Andrews, in 1211. Pitmilly House was demolished after the direct line of the Monypennys died out and a hotel venture failed.

East Neuk

At Kingsbarns the visitor travelling south enters the 'East Neuk of Fife' celebrated in the poem by William Drummond of Hawthornden (1585–1649) entitled *'Polemo-middinia inter Vitarvam et Nebernam'*, bynamed 'The Battle of the Dunghill' (1684). Thus this part of Fife was designated the 'East Neuk' from at least the seventeenth century. It was also celebrated in the humorous song 'Auld Gudeman ye're a drunken carle' by Sir James Boswell. Today the East Neuk is understood to cover land in the old parishes of Kingsbarns, Crail, Kilrenny, Anstruther, Pittenweem, St Monans and Carnbee.

KINGSEAT

An old mining village now being absorbed in the expanding private dwellings of Dunfermline's eastward elevation.

KINGSKETTLE

Once on the post carriage route between Edinburgh, Dundee and Aberdeen, Kingskettle is in the ancient parish of Kettle, and formerly bynamed Lathrisk. These lands of 'Katul' belonged to the Crown and the name developed as Kingskettle. The property hereabouts was ceded by Malcolm IV to Duncan, Earl of Fife, on his marraige to the king's neice Ada, and remained in the succeeding earls' possession until forfeiture in 1437. To the south are the lands of Chapel, properly Chapel-Kettle, taking its name from a dependancy of the Augustinian priory of St Andrews, acres that James Stewart, Commendator of the Priory, disponed to the Arnot family in 1558.

Today the village nestles by the railway linking Perth and Edinburgh, opened in 1847 by the North British Railway Co. The village retains its neat stone villas and cottages, mostly of the eighteenth and nineteenth centuries, set around a nucleus of the elegant 'Tudor' Gothic church of 1831–2 which replaced the older church of St Ethernaseus, *c.* 1636, which itself succeeded the church dedicated by Bishop David de Bernham of St Andrews in 1243. The former manse dates from 1792. The earliest parish church is said to have been that of Lathrisk dating from the fourteenth century, now thought to have been part of Lathrisk House of 1710–80; there are sites of pre-Reformation chapels too at Clatto and Chapel-Kettle.

The people of Kingskettle once found employment as weavers, quarriers and processors of lime at the works at Forthar; today most commute to a variety of employment elsewhere.

A parish school was erected in 1834 and a primary school in 1876.

Near Kettlebridge once stood Bankton House, the long vanished home of James Russell, one of the murderers of Archbishop James Sharp in 1679. Clatto Tower was home to the Seaton family; they were traditionally known as notorious robbers and murderers, highwaymen on the Cupar–Kinghorn road. Members of the Seaton family, it is said, attacked James IV and his small escort on the road, but were subsequently tried and executed.

KINLOCH

A hamlet historically connected to Collessie. Said to have been within the properties of Roger de Quincy, Earl of Winchester (d.1264), High Constable of Scotland to Alexander III. Kinloch House is an 1859 edifice incorporating an older building, and includes interior alterations of 1881 and 1923.

KIRKLAND

This village, once known as the hamlet of Kirkland of Methil, has long merged with Methil proper, but is remembered as a district and in such names as Kirkland High School (1959), Kirkland Weir and Kirkland Dam on the River Leven. The village owed its development, within the ancient parish of Wemyss, as a source of water power for colliery works, then to the spinning and bleaching of yarn and the manufacturing of linen cloth by the firm of Aislabie Nelson and Co.

KIRKTON

A small village now merged as a district of Burntisland. Some historians believe that this was the *Parva Kingorne*, 'Little Kinghorn', mentioned in medieval documents as having a church rededicated in 1243 by David de Bernham of St Andrews. Sited in modern Church Street, St Serf's is the successor of de Bernham's church and was abandoned around 1595 when a new parish church was built for Burntisland folk. In medieval times the lands around were within the possession of the abbots of Dunfermline.

KIRKTON OF BALMERINO (see: BALMERINO)

KIRKTON OF LARGO (see: LARGO, UPPER)

LADYBANK

Known prior to the twelfth century as Moss of Monagray, the area now recognised as Ladybank was exploited as a peat-cutting source by the monks of the Order of Tiron at Lindores Abbey. This privilege had been granted to them by landholder Earl Roger de Quincy (d.1264), Constable of Scotland. The monks called their workings

'Our Lady's Bog'. Prior to the construction of burns and drainage channels like the great Rossie Drain from the mid-eighteenth century, the area was very marshy with a loch (drained 1740). The name Lady's Bog was changed to Ladybank when the North British Railway (later LNER) junction was being planned 1847–8. Today the name Monkstown, a district of Ladybank alongside the B938 – and the only part of Ladybank to precede the railway construction of the late 1840s – is the sole memory of the holy brothers of Lindores, although Monkstown only came into being when the whole of nearby Kinloch's inhabitants were transferred here at the beginning of the nineteenth century.

Before the coming of the railway the extant village (that is, Monkstown) had no buildings of great age. Ladybank was made a burgh in 1878 and was noted for its linen and maltings; Ladybank Maltings were demolished in 1986. The parish church in Church Street dates from 1874–6, and Ladybank Pumping Station, in Beeches Road, from 1908. Ladybank railway station remains a fine example of a largely unaltered piece of nineteenth-century railway architecture.

LANGDYKE

An agricultural hamlet flanked north-east by Devon Wood and Devon Common, and north-west by Drummy Wood and Milldeans Wood. It is likely that these medieval hunting lands were within the portion given by one Merleswain, son of Colbain, to the Augustinian priory of St Andrews around 1150, thereafter within the barony of Fithkill, in the favour of the earls of Rothes.

LARGO, LOWER

Set along the rim of Largo Bay, the fishing village once known as Seatown of Largo had its own station on the old LNER line, and includes the old hamlets of Temple and Drummochy. The village became a barony in 1513; there were weavers here in the eighteenth century. Largo St David's Parish Church, Main Street, dates from 1871–2. There is a mixture of modern and nineteenth-century housing, with two hotels of note, the Crusoe Hotel of c. 1850, once a granary, and the eighteenth-century Railway Inn. The 1856–7 four-arch Railway Viaduct is a distinctive feature of the Valley of the Keil Burn. At the mouth of the Keil Burn is sited the old harbour, with

The quays of Seatown of Largo, now known as Lower Largo. This single street village was home to eigthteenth-century weavers and fishermen and was busy in the nineteenth-century as a steamboat service station for Newhaven. [*Alexander B. Paterson*]

*c.*1770 pier, from where steamboats plied to Newhaven. Once the quay saw the loading of coal, salt and sandstone for Rotterdam and wood from Norway. Visitors cannot fail to notice Stewart Burnett's 1885 statue of Alexander Selkirk (1676–1721), who became the inspiration for Daniel Defoe's *Robinson Crusoe*; the statue at 101 Main Street marks the site of a thatched cottage said to be the birthplace of Selkirk. The village has a variety of eighteenth- and nineteenth-century dwellings.

LARGO, UPPER

When Largo Law the mist cloth wear,
Let Kellie Law for storms prepare.
(*Local weather lore*)

Known also as Kirkton of Largo, the village sits at the foot of conical Largo Law, and is associated with the hamlets of Backmuir of Gilston and Woodside. Largo was given over to the monastery at North

Berwick by Duncan, Earl of Fife, in the twelfth century. Largo Estate was long the home of the Durham family of ruined Largo House (1750). Colonel Sir Andrew Durham was prominent at the court of Charles II and was appointed Lyon King of Arms in 1660. The barony of Largo was confirmed on Scottish naval commander Sir Andrew Wood by James III in 1482. Within the old policies of Largo House is the 'castle' inhabited by Sir Andrew, which some historians have identified with a former dower house of the queens of Scotland.

The parish church is substantially seventeenth century with a tower of 1628 and chancel of 1623, the whole being incorporated into a cruciform church built 1816–17 and expanded 1826. A manse dates from 1770 and 1837. The Largo Stone in the churchyard shows that this area once saw extensive Celtic activity. Kirkton of Largo former primary school dates from 1890–91. Woods Hospital, Woodlaw Park, was set up out of a legacy of the Woods of Largo for the succour of certain 'indigent and enfeebled persons of the name of Wood'; building commenced in 1665 for habitation in 1667. The newer hospital buildings on the site date from 1830. Largo's chief industry was formerly the manufacture of linen, and there were once extensive bleaching greens in the village. Housing developments are fast making Upper Largo, Lower Largo and Lundin Links into a single entity. Upper Largo is still linked to the sea by a footpath known as 'The Serpentine'.

> The battle fiercely it was fought
> Near to the Craig of Bass;
> When we next fight the English loons,
> May nae waur come to pass.

Thus was 'local hero' Sir Andrew Wood celebrated; in 1499 he captured the English Admiral Stephen Bull and three ships using James III's vessels the *Yellow Carvel* and the *Flower*, off the Bass Rock. One more Largo naval hero is well known among villagers: Sir Philip Charles Henderson Calderwood Durham (1763–1845). By 1781 he was acting lieutenant aboard *HMS Victory*. The next year he was aboard the 108-ton *HMS Royal George*; on 29 August, while undergoing repairs off Spithead, the vessel careened over and was lost. William Cowper wrote of the tragedy:

> Toll for the brave!
> The brave that are no more
> All sunk beneath the wave,
> Fast by their native shore.

The 1816–17 parish church of Kirkton of Largo, known today as Upper Largo, incorporates a tower of 1628, and dominates the village in this scene of around 1840. [*Author's collection*]

Eight hundred died with their captain Rear-Admiral Richard Kempenfelt, but Durham was saved. He was present at the naval campaigns at Gibraltar, Cape Spartel, Tory Island and Cape Finisterre. At Trafalgar in 1805, his great triumph was in trying to save the 74-gun French frigate *L'Aigle* from going down. His list of exploits stretched from the Leewards to Guadaloupe and he was made Admiral in 1815.

LARGOWARD

This small village lies in the old parish of Kilconquhar on sloping land alongside the A915 St Andrews to Kirkcaldy road. It has a core of three main public buildings: the parish church (1835), a village hall (1907) and the primary school of around 1840. It was once a mining village (cf. Radernie and Lathones), and enters history as supplying fuel to the court of James VI at Falkland Palace; mining ceased in the 1920s. Writing in 1792 the Rev. Alexander Small of Kilconquhar noted that thirty-seven 'tolerably regular and industrious' Largoward colliers were working 'hard and soft coal' for James Calderwood Durham of Largo House. Nearby Gilston House dates from the 1870s.

LASSODIE

The village of Lassodie, in the old parish of Beath, enters recorded history in 1593–4. That year James VI conferred upon his wife, Anne of Denmark, certain secular landholdings in Fife and portions of ecclesiastical land that had once been in the ownership of the abbey of Dunfermline. This gift included 'Lessody Eister and Wester', the 'Mill of Lessody' and accompanying mill lands. By 1606 the Lassodie properties had fallen to William, Earl of Morton, and a series of other holders followed. Lassodie developed in the nineteenth century as a mining village.

LATHONES

This is a small hamlet set along the A915 St Andrews to Kirkcaldy road centred upon an inn, with the Lathockar Burn to its southern edge. It was situated in Cameron parish from 1645 and is a remnant of a trio of mining settlements (cf. Radernie and Largoward). Coal from its defunct pits was once transported to the royal palace at Falkland; coal was still hewn hereabouts until the 1920s for local mine owners like the Lindsays. Its landscape is still pitted with shafts and weathered shale heaps, across land which once belonged, mainly, to the Augustinian priory of St Andrews, and kept as medieval runs for game. This area was deemed to have a healthy climate; the Cameron minister, the Rev. John Mair, reported in 1793 that his flock included several octo- and nonagenarians.

LESLIE

Flax-spinning, bleaching, papermaking and a vulcanite works all contributed to the development of Leslie, once called Fythkill, or Fettykill, which was the centre of an eponymous parish. On the River Leven and at the southern elevation of the Lomond Hills, Leslie began as a village burgh of barony in 1458 in a holding under the Leslie family, the earls of Rothes, with the right to hold two annual fairs in spring and autumn for the sale of horses and cattle. At Michaelmas fair, reported the Rev. George Willis of Leslie in 1792, large quantities of eels were taken from the Leven; once Leslie eels were paid as tax to the land superiors, the Augustinian monks of Inchcolm Abbey. Between 1865–1975 Leslie was a 'police burgh' and still retains a separate character from nearby sprawling 'new town' of Glenrothes.

The earls of Rothes' power-base was Leslie House – 'Villa de Rothes' – (now a retirement home), built by John Leslie, 6th Earl of Rothes (later 1st Duke of Rothes), Lord Chancellor of Scotland, during 1667–72. Although described by Daniel Defoe in 1707 as the 'Glory of Fife', the house suffered serious fire damage in 1763; the repaired section of 1765–7 forms the present house. The Rothes were descended from Fleming Bartholomew, who secured Crown lands in Aberdeenshire. His descendants were prominent figures at the royal court. In 1283 Norman de Lesly obtained a grant of the land of Fythkill from Alexander III; George de Lesly of Rothes was created Earl of Rothes in 1457, by which time the name of Fythkill had been changed to Leslie.

Leslie Church was erected in 1819–21 on the site of a medieval church prominent in the area by 1591; the church was extended in 1868–69. The manse predates the church, being built 1811–13. Leslie Church – 'Christ's Kirk on the Green' – has in its graveyard the mausolea of the Rothes and Douglas families whose activities gave Leslie its early place in history. The location is given as the traditional setting of the popular Scottish poem *Christis Kirk on the Grene*, attributed by some to James I and by others to James V. The poem refers to Leslie wappinshaw, or fair, by the church, which earned medieval fame for its distinctive high jinks:

> Was never in Scotland heard or seen
> Sic dancing and deray;
> Nowther at Falkland on the green,
> Nor Peblis* at the play
> As was of woers, as I ween,
> At Christ's Kirk on ane day ...
>
> * Peebles

The character of Leslie village folk was assessed by the Rev. Willis as 'sober, honest and industrious'. He went on:

> In the church of Leslie no person is ever seen in rags. The young men wear coats of English cloth, fancy vests &c and the young women, printed and white cottons, silk cloaks and bonnets ... Their furniture also is much better. About thirty years ago [c.1760] ... there was not 6 clocks in the parish, and now there is not a house in Leslie where there is not either a clock or watch.

The old heart of Leslie is represented by The Green, where a war memorial of around 1920 stands on the supposed site of an old mercat cross. Behind is placed a weathered-grooved stone which local tradition associates with bull-baiting. Around are eighteenth- and nineteenth-century buildings. The chapmen – itinerant pedlars and carriers – are said to have had their headquarters at Leslie where they met on the Green for sport and recreation; new members were initiated in a ducking ceremony.

Neighbours of Leslie to the west worthy of mention are the early seventeenth-century tower-house of Strathendry Castle, built for Thomas Forrester and his wife Isobel Learmonth, with additions built for the subsequent owner Sir Edward Douglas in 1699; the whole was remodelled in 1824, 1845 and 1943. Strathendry House dates from 1824 and was built for Robert Douglas.

Local village gossip put an interesting spin on a saying concerning the Leslies, which ran: 'Ask no questions of the Leslies'. A dark meaning was locally attached to this phrase as the Leslies were concerned in the murder of Cardinal Archbishop David Beaton. The prelate was stabbed by Norman Leslie at St Andrews Castle in 1546 and George, 4th Earl of Rothes, was tried for his part in the assassination conspiracy; he was acquitted. It paid to give the Leslies a wide berth.

LETHAM

Once known for its fair, during the first week of June, although this and Letham's substantial market have long been discontinued. In 1840 John Leighton described the fair where 'a procession usually takes place, and the keepers of stalls for the sale of toys and sweetmeats, continue their attendance'. Letham, which still has its open green, belonged to the archbishopric of St Andrews and the archbishop rented out portions of the surrounding land; in 1551 a grant of lands was made to one Elizabeth Lindsay and her family with a part rent of 'four thraives of straw' for the archbishop's use at his Tower of Monimail (a thraive was a measure of cut straw of around twelve sheaves). Lethan barony (with Monimail) was acquired in 1587 by Sir Robert Melville of Murdocairney (Baron Melville of Monimail, 1616).

Letham supported a parochial school, built in 1804 and extended in 1820, a parish library and a brewery for 'table and small beer', but most folk were employed in agriculture. Today Letham is usually described as a 'large hillside hamlet', and is largely made up of eighteenth- and nineteenth-century slated single-storey cottages, with a few pantiled, but much altered. In the area are some interesting doocots of seventeenth- and eighteenth-century origin; the two at School Brae are lectern type. It has developed as a dormitory village.

To the south-east of Letham three medieval sites are worthy of mention. At Balgarvie a now vanished castle was beseiged and razed to the ground by the English army led by Sir John Pettsworth when he was marching on Cupar in the wars of Robert the Bruce. Again at Uthrogle, in lands formerly owned by the earls of Fife, a leper hospital is recorded with chapel dedicated to St John the Baptist; it flourished 1394–1462 and was annexed to the long-demolished Trinity Hospital beside the College of the Holy Trinity, Edinburgh, for the maintenance of the Trinity bedesmen. The hospital was in the gift of the Dowager Queen Mary of Guelders. Along the road from Uthrogle, towards Cupar, lies ruined Carslogie House. In its previous form as Carslogie Tower it appears several times in Fife's history. By the early eighteenth century the property was in the hands of the Clephane family who had held the barony for almost seven centuries. Sir Mark de Clephane swore fealty to Edward I in 1296. It is said that Alan de Clephane fought for Robert I at Bannockburn; in the battle his left hand was severed and the king ordered that an artificial limb be made for him. This steel hand subsequently became a family heirloom and was in the possession of Margaret Clephane, Marchioness of Northampton (1793–1830) whose guardian was Sir Walter Scott. The famous 'Battle Horn of Carslogie' was mentioned by Sir Walter in his *Border Antiquities*. The 'Jug Tree' (from the Scots *jougs*, a hinged iron collar attached by a chain and locked round an offender's neck) was long pointed out as a place of punishment at Carslogie.

Also to the south-east of Letham is the classical mansion of Over Rankeillour, dating from 1796–1800, within an estate which before the sixteenth century was the property of the Rankeillours of that Ilk, encompassing (in 1540) a 'tower, manor, fortalice [and] mills'. This latter messuage had fallen to the Sibbald family, whose most prominent denizen was Sir Robert Sibbald of Kipps (1641–1722), historian, royal geographer and physician to Charles II. Although the medieval tower of Rankeillour has now vanished, the estate was much improved in the eighteenth century by the Hopes of Rankeillour; Lieutenant General Sir John Hope (1765–1823), later 4th Earl of Hopetoun, built the extant mansion.

LEUCHARS

Long before the supporters of the monarchs of the House of Dunkeld merged in the peaceful invasion of the Anglo-Normans to choose the rush-strewn wetlands of Leuchars as a strategic base, the area was a wild, marshy, enchanted and isolated region which the medieval chroniclers filled with *diaboli, urses et bos priminginius* (devils, bears and oxen). Thus the area now known as Morton Lochs, Tentsmuir Forest and Reres Wood was a place of early habitation in Fife from the Stone Age. By the time a village was evolving at Leuchars the surrounding area was inhabited by shipwrecked mariners and a sanctuary for vagabonds and outlaws.

Records show that the Lordship of Leuchars was established by 1153 in the reign of Malcolm IV, The Maiden, in the name of one Ness of Locres. Some time around the 1170s the land was inherited by Arabella, daughter of Ness, who married Robert de Quinci (d.1192) of the Anglo-Norman family which held the manor of Bushby; this was formerly in the Northamptonshire earldom of Prince David who became King David I (r.1124–53). Robert de Quinci died in the Third Crusade. His son Seyer de Quinci (d.1219) became a benefactor of the Augustinian priory of St Andrews, and in 1210 was elevated to the earldom of Winchester; he was one of the barons who extracted Magna Carta from King John in 1215. Through Seyer's son, Roger, the De Quincis strengthened their place in Scottish politics and court circles when he became Great Constable of Scotland.

Roger de Quinci was benefactor to the Fife monasteries of Balmerino and Lindores and his descendants held the Lordship of Leuchars until the fourteenth century whereupon it fell to the Crown and was gifted to various individuals.

Tradition has it that the castle of Leuchars, on its oval motte and guarded by a deep ditch and swamp to the north-west of the modern village, was built by Ness and became the chief residence in Scotland of the de Quincis. Attacked and demolished by the English army brought to Scotland by Amyer de Valence, Earl of Pembroke, in 1327, it was rebuilt to evolve as a medieval tower-house. In the eighteenth century the castle was acquired by Robert Lindsay of Balcarres who demolished it in the early 1800s to use as a quarry. To the south-west of the site the castle doocot of 1661 survives.

Leuchars has been a site of Christian worship since the tenth century. Near to where the present church is located a Celtic chapel

Maids at the courtyard well of Earlshall Castle, 1892. The castle estate provided work for many who lived in nearby Leuchars village. [*Baron and Baroness of Earlshall*]

dedicated to St Bunoc, or Bunan, was founded around 900 with an associated holy well. Between 1183–7, Ness gifted a church to the Augustinian priory of St Andrews, and his descendants funded the foundation and a serving priest. The church was dedicated to St Athernase – an Irish saint, a contemporary of St Columba – in 1244 by David de Bernham, Bishop of St Andrews. Leuchars Church at Schoolhill remains as a fine example of Romanesque architecture completed around the late twelfth century; the chancel arch and vaulted apse retain the original form. In the seventeenth century the original timber roof of the apse was replaced and an octagonal bell-turret erected topped by a lead weathervane. The nave was much altered down the centuries with its modern form dating from 1857–8. As well as an interesting range of sixteenth-century gravestones in the churchyard, the church interior sheltered several important graveslabs. One to Sir Robert Carnegy, of 1565, has fine lettering, while that of Sir William Bruce of Earlshall (1584) has elaborately carved designs; the slab for Agnes Lindsay (1635) has an almost lifesize carved figure of the deceased.

In 1792 the Rev. Kettle, the parish minister, described Leuchars as 'a pleasant healthy country village' consequent upon the excavation

An ariel view of Leuchars taken in the 1930s, showing how the village developed around the parish church of St Athernase, 1183–7, at Schoolhill. Once the village was surrounded by marshes, drained in the 1790s; the village became an important railway junction from 1848. [*Staralp*]

of a 'great drain' which dried the surrounding land and thereby reduced the incidence of 'intermittent fevers' which dogged the village from early spring to late autumn. Today Leuchars still has a village core which is largely eighteenth century with Victorian and Edwardian additions. From being a slow agricultural community, its character was greatly altered with the coming of the railway in 1848, the development of the link to St Andrews in 1852 and the evolution of a Royal Air Force base in 1920. The Royal Engineers brought aeronautics to Leuchars in 1911 when they experimented with balloons. During the First World War an airfield took shape between the village and the Eden Estuary, where the Royal Navy commanded a Fleet Training School taken over by the RAF. By 1938 Leuchars airfield became fully operational as a base for Coastal Command; in 1950 it transferred to Fighter Command and eventually to Strike Command in 1968.

The largest surviving early building in Leuchars parish is Earlshall. In the fourteenth century this area abutting Leuchars village was the estate of the Duke of Albany, as Earl of Fife. The castle was constructed in 1546 by Sir William Bruce and its core is a sixteenth-century L-plan tower-house with seventeenth-century additions. The gatehouse was built around 1900. In time the whole passed to the Hendersons of Fordell who sold the castle and estate in 1852. The buildings fell into decay but were acquired by R.W.R. Mackenzie of Stormontfield, who commissioned Sir Robert Lorimer to restore them during 1891–8. A private house, the castle still displays its distinctive long gallery with painted ceilings showing the arms of the principal families of Scotland and a myriad of mythical and fabulous beasts. Mary Queen of Scots visited the castle in 1561. Outside, Earlshall gardens contain topiary yews in the form of chessmen, again to Lorimer's designs.

Just to the north of Leuchars village lies Pitlethie; here was the site of a royal hunting lodge. It is said that James VI particularly enjoyed hunting with hawks in the nearby forests.

LEVEN

Historically Leven, on its eponymous river emptying into Largo Bay, is within the old seaboard parish of Scoonie, and is traditionally the east end of Fife's industrial belt. Up to at least 1546, Leven was referred to in charters as *Levynsmouth*, with spelling variations; by the sixteenth century it was a flourishing fishing village. Charters of the period suggest that the habitation and its harbour belonged to the archdiocese of St Andrews. In 1609 Archbishop George Gledstanes granted title *inter alia* of 'Leven, porte and heavin of Leven' to George Lauder of Bass, whose impecunious family sold out to Sir Alexander Gibson of Liberton; in 1619 he added Leven to his recently purchased Durie estate and thus Leven became a burgh of barony.

From around 1435 Leven harbour –'The Port of Markinch' – had some importance, and saw the unloading of meat carcasses bought for the royal court when based at Falkland Palace. In 1602 Leven was banned from importing or exporting any goods, so great was the contraband in these parts. By the 1830s Leven harbour had fallen into increasing decay, but a rebuilding programme was enacted during 1876–80. The harbour declined with the construction of new docks at Methil, and by 1910 the whole had silted up and were closed.

From around the 1790s, Leven was a place of handloom weavers, but by the 1890s had diversified: flax-spinning, seed-crushing, sawmilling, rope-spinning and brickmaking were among the occupations, and there was an iron foundry. By the First World War, Leven had become a centre of mining and engineering works. Large postwar housing estates altered Leven's village character.

The parish of Scoonie is remembered in Old Scoonie Parish Church at Scoonie Brae, now but a roofless fragment. It recalls how this church was granted to the Culdees of Loch Leven by Tuadal, Bishop of St Andrews, in the 1060s; the church became redundant when a new church was built at Leven in 1775; the ruins of this original church became the burial vault of the families who dwelt at Durie House. Hereabouts from the twelfth century a hamlet grew that became modern Leven. Durie House (1762) recalls the lairdship through which Leven became a burgh of barony. Today Leven is a part of an urban sprawl linking its boundaries with Methil and Buckhaven.

Two miles north of Leven lay the medieval estate of Aithernie, granted to the nuns of North Berwick by the Earl of Fife in 1160. The convent held the lands until 1588 because the title was held by prioress Margaret Home who petitioned the king to have the lands disponed to her relative Sir Alexander Home (d.1608), a prominent member of the Scottish court and James VI's ambassador to England. Aithernie Castle is now a ruin.

LIMEKILNS

Brewing, fishing, salt panning, soap-making, ropemaking and some shipbuilding gave Limekilns its industrial history as well as the processing of lime that gave it its name. The harbour of Limekilns was once the port of medieval Dunfermline and its fifteenth-century timber pier was replaced in stone in the sixteenth century. Brucehaven harbour of c.1750 was constructed for the coal trade. Nowadays piers like Capernaum serve as moorings for pleasure boats. In Academy Square the sixteenth-century King's Cellar stored provisions for the palace of Dunfermline; its doorway of 1581 bears the arms of the Commendator of Dunfermline, Robert Pitcairn. Today Limekilns is a place of retirement homes and commuter houses.

LINDORES

Set near the Loch of Lindores, the village probably developed from a hamlet surrounding a now vanished castle, once the property of

The Grange of Lindores, a village that owed its birth to the nearby Lindores Abbey, founded in 1191 for the Monks of the Order of Tiron, by David, Earl of Huntingdon. Here were situated the abbey cereal barns, and this Victorian print provides a good example of a Fife thatched village. [*Author's collection*]

David Barclay, Lord of Brechin in the fourteenth century, and then the earls of Fife. By the sixteenth century the castle was in the ownership of the Mackgills of Nether Rankeillour who let it fall into ruin when they built their new mansion. The chronicler 'Blind Harry the Minstrel' (fl.1470–92) recalls that it was to Lindores Castle that Sir William Wallace retired after the nearby Battle of Black Earnside (1298). Here Wallace defeated an English army under Aymer de Valance, Earl of Pembroke. This was Hyrneside of medieval parlance where Earl David of Huntingdon had his red sandstone quarry from which the ashlar of Lindores Abbey was hewn; the battlefield and quarry site is on the modern farm estate of Parkhill. Local tradition has it that Lindores also saw another battle in 621 when Cinioch MacLuchtren, King of the Picts, was struggling against Edwin of Northumbria.

Lindores is within the old parish of Abdie, and across the loch from the extant village is Abdie Church; in monastic times a now vanished hamlet abutted the church known as 'Auld Lindores'. The old parish church of Abdie was dedicated to St Magridin, and was consecrated by David de Bernham, Bishop of St Andrews, in 1242. Known in medieval times as 'Ebedyn', the church was a gift of Earl David to Lindores Abbey, and was served by a monastic chaplain. It remains a roofless shell with reparations of 1803 and 1856, although it was abandoned for worship in 1827. The seventeenth-century north transept is the burial place of the Balfours of Denmylne. The church's seventeenth-century gateway is flanked by the Offertory House of 1748. Abdie House of 1839–40 is the former manse, and Abdie Parish Church dates from 1827. A prominent former land-owner of Lindores lies buried in the churchyard: Sir Frederick Lewis Maitland (1777–1839), son of the 6th Earl of Lauderdale, was captain of the British warship *HMS Bellerephon*, which took the defeated Napoleon on board in 1815 before transferring him to the *Northumberland*, bound for exile on St Helena. As Rear-Admiral Maitland of Lindores House the erstwhile captain died on his ship off India.

It is interesting to note that there were once three lochs between Abdie Church and Dunbog, but Lindores Loch is the only one remaining, the haunt of anglers and wild birds.

South-east of Lindores lies the site of the mansion of Inchrye Abbey, once set within fine lawns and woods, which was the home of the Rt Rev. William Scot Wilson, Episcopal Bishop of Glasgow and Galloway (d.1888). Inchrye Lodge dates from 1827 and Lindores House from 1820.

LINKTOWN

Part of the western suburbs of Kirkcaldy, this was made a burgh of barony in 1663 and annexed to Kirkcaldy in 1876. Its character has now been altered by areas of new housing, portions developed on the site of the Seafield Colliery of 1954; production ceased in 1988. At the edge of the old mine policies lies Seafield Tower, the sixteenth-century power-base of the Moutray family. Abbotshall School, of 1890–91, recalls in name the old parish of Abbotshall, itself named after the country dwelling of the abbots of Dunfermline. This monastic estate developed into Raith House, a villa built for Alexander Melville, Lord Raith, Treasurer-Depute of Scotland, in 1693–6; the house was remodelled in 1785. Nearby Beveridge Park was laid out in 1891, a result of the bequest of floorcovering manufacturer Provost Michael Beveridge, a prominent Kirkcaldy benefactor. Once the lodge (1790) by the gateway to the park was the main entrance to

Raith House. Here too the Tiel Burn is crossed by the Linktown railway viaduct of 1845–7.

At Linktown was the now vanished Gladney House, off Bute Wynd. This was the birthplace of the architects Robert and James Adam, whose mother Mary was a Robertson of Gladney.

LOCHGELLY

Set within the old parish of Auchterhouse, Lochgelly remains in Fife history mainly for its collieries and iron works, and is clustered around the A910 Dunfermline–Kirkcaldy road. Records show that Lochgelly village was a portion of the Boswells' barony of Glassmount in 1485, and there were mines here from the thirteenth century, owned by men such as Sir John Wemyss of Wemyss. Modern Lochgelly has its roots in a sixteenth-century hamlet of thatched huts. The mansion house of Lochgelly, its village and estate belonged to the Kininmonths and then the earls of Minto by marriage. In 1877 Lochgelly became a burgh.

Loch Gelly lies to the south-west of the village core and was known in medieval times for the efficacy of its leeches. When agriculture played a more prominent role, during the eighteenth century and the beginning of the nineteenth century, Lochgelly was known for its cattle markets, and as a winter encampment for gipsies. Around 1836 the forerunners of the Lochgelly Iron Co. (1851) acquired a lease of mineral rights which in 1872 developed into the Lochgelly Iron and Coal Co.; the coal workings are now defunct but Lochgelly once had seven pits.

The oldest extant place of worship is St Andrews Church, Bank Street, of 1854–5, enlarged in 1915, although a new church had been established here in 1789, preceded by a manse of 1784. Ecclesiastical records suggest that a church was established hereabouts and gifted to the monks of the Celtic foundation of Lochleven by Fothad II (1059–93), the last Celtic bishop of St Andrews; this church, now vanished, was rededicated by David de Bernham, Bishop of St Andrews in 1244.

Overall the character of Lochgelly reflects its mining past. The spirit of the mining community expressed in such buildings as the Miners' Welfare and War Memorial Institute of 1923–5 in Main Street, and the late nineteenth- and early twentieth-century colliers' dwellings augmented by local authority schemes. Children once had a reason to dislike the name Lochgelly as it was the commercial name of a locally made hard leather belt used for discipline in school. When the sale of liquor was restricted by the Forbes Mackenzie Act, crossed pipes in a Lochgelly shop meant that the shopkeeper was willing to slake the thirst of passers-by. Greyhounds and pigeon racing were the traditional pastimes of the mining communities hereabouts, but up to the First World War at least Lochgelly offered a darker diversion – cockfighting, which had been illegal since 1849. Standing at 606 ft, Lochgelly is the highest settlement in Fife.

LOGIE

Ancient Logie-Murdoch estate was within royal hunting lands. During the reign of Robert III (r.1390–1406) the lands of Logie were granted to Sir John Wemyss of Reres. Sir John was the patron of Prior Andrew Wyntoun (c.1355–1422) the Augustinian canon who was head of the priory of St Serf's, Lochleven and produced the informative *Orygynale Cronikil of Scotland*. In his *Minstrelsy of the Scottish Border* Sir Walter Scott offers the ballad 'The Laird of Logie', which tells of an adventure concerning one John Wemyss of Logie, a gallant at the court of James IV. At one time Logie was known for its handloom weavers, but today it is a settlement made up of a church, manse (now Lucklaw House, 1815), old parish school (1858) and a farm. Medieval Logie Church was a dependant of Balmerino Abbey and was assumed into the Presbyterian ascendancy in 1562; by 1590 it had fallen into great disrepair. The more modern church was built in 1826 and altered in 1893.

It is likely that Sir John Wemyss constructed the baronial fortalice of Cruivie Castle when his castle of Reres was destroyed by David, Duke of Rothesay, in 1402. Today the roofless ruin near South Straiton dates from the late fifteenth and early sixteenth century and forms an L-plan tower. Cruivie was the centrepiece of the old barony of Logie-Murdoch and by 1539 it fell to the estates passed to the earls of Southesk but were forfeited when James, 5th Earl of Southesk, was involved in the 1715 rebellion.

LOW VALLEYFIELD

The estate of Valleyfield developed into the mining settlement of High Valleyfield, which sits on the hill above the older Low Valleyfield, fronting the shores of the Forth overlooking Torry Bay. The estate of Valleyfield belonged to Sir Robert Preston who employed Humphry Repton (1752–1818), one of the great names of the English art of landscape gardening, to improve his parkland. Preston's house was demolished in 1918 and much of Repton's landscaping is irredeemably lost, destroyed by its later owner, the East Fife Coal Co., who bought the estate in 1907 for its mineral rights. Valleyfield is still remembered in mining lore for the pit disaster of 1939 when thirty-five miners lost their lives.

LUCKLAWHILL

Within the old parish of Logie, and the runs of the royal medieval hunt, Lucklawhill has developed as a scattered hamlet around the western mid-base of Lucklaw Hill abutting Balmullo.

LUMPHINNANS

An old mining settlement adjacent to Lochgelly on the A910 Dunfermline–Kirkcaldy road, in the parish of Ballingry. Once divided into North and South Lumphinnans, this was the property severally of such as the earls of Minto and the marquis of Zetland and formed part of the barony of Lochore. The Cowdenbeath Colliery Co. (taken over by the Fife Coal Co. in 1896) gave Lumphinnans its reason for existance, although John Bleau's *Atlas* of 1654 shows a now vanished church by the burn which would be likely to have an associate hamlet. Lumphinnans United Free Church of old dates from 1900 and was subsequently known as the North Church, Perth Road, Cowdenbeath, while Lumphinnans Primary School of 1892–3, 1901–03 and 1909 is sited in Main Street.

LUNDIN LINKS

Housing developments have made Lundin Links merge, at its eastern end, with Lower Largo. Once Lundin Links was dubbed the 'Scottish Riviera' by local hoteliers and is a part of the old parish of Largo. To its west end stands ruined Lundin Tower, all that remains of the Lundin estates founded by Philip de Lundin in the reign of Malcolm IV (1153–65). The lands passed to the Erskines of Torry and the Wemysses in 1840, and thence to the Gilmours of Montrave, but the

Montrave House

associated mansion was demolished in 1876. Lundin Doocot was originally an eighteenth-century laundry converted in the nineteenth century. There is a fine range of middle-class nineteenth-century villas while the Lundin Links Hotel dates from 1900.

Set within the golf course of the Ladies Golf Club are the celebrated standing stones associated in local tradition with the Druids. Today Lundin Links sports holiday and dormitory housing with its golf course as part of the infrastructure; a golf course was first set out in 1868 and restructured in 1877. Associate habitations with separate village roots are Lundin Mill and Drumochie.

LUTHRIE

The ancient barony of Luthrie was once Crown property, with grants given to such as John Murray, barber-surgeon to James V. The area also supported the estates of the House of Luthrie and the mansions of Carphin and Parbroath. Carphin House as a late eighteenth- and early nineteenth-century edifice survives. These estates flourished in the fourteenth century. The now vanished Parbroath was the seat of the Seton family, whose scion Sir Alexander Seton, Governor of Berwick-upon-Tweed, held the castle and town there against Edward III in 1333, despite the king's triumph at the nearby Battle of Halidon Hill.

The church of Luthrie (Creich Parish Church) was begun 1829–30. Confusingly for visitors, old Creich Parish Church stands up the hill beyond Brunton. In the vestibule of the parish church stands an early fifteenth-century gravestone showing a knight in plate armour and his lady, for David Barclay of Luthrie and his wife Helen Douglas. Luthrie supported a parish school. In 1840 the schoolmaster's fees were quoted as: 'per quarter, for English reading 2s [10p], for reading with writing 2s 6d [12 and a half p], for these with arithmetic 3s [15p], and for Latin 5s [25p]'.

The famous Rev. Alexander Henderson was born at Luthrie in 1583. Educated at St Andrews Henderson was a prominent cleric within the Episcopalian church, but turned Presbyterian to promote the National Covenant. In 1640 he was elected Rector of Edinburgh University and as chaplain to Charles I played a prominent diplomatic role in church affairs. He died in 1646.

MARKINCH

The village from which Markinch developed spread out from the parish church situated at Kirk Brae. This much-restored church is on the site of an earlier one dedicated to St Drostan, which had been gifted by the Earl of Fife to the Augustinian priory of St Andrews around 1203. Even so, historians maintain that the early medieval church was a successor of a missionary chapel set up in the seventh century by Abbot Drostan of Deer, nephew of St Columba. The Norman tower remains after the rebuild of 1786, but the spire was altered in 1807 and the interior was reconstructed in 1883. At the church gate is the 1875 session house into which is inserted a thirteenth-century foliaceous capital and a niche canopy of later date. Though Christianity has flourished at Markinch for 800 years, this place was once called Dalgynch, the pagan Pictish capital of Fife.

Chartered by Charles II at a burgh of barony in 1673, Markinch has hilly elevations of note; the sister hill to the one on which the parish church is set, Markinch Hill, has cultivation terraces suggesting medieval activity. Next to this, set on a banking to the left of Stobbcross Road out of Markinch, is Stobb Cross, which is thought to have stood at the entrance to St Drostan's Church. The monument is considered by historians to be a *gyrth* cross marking the boundary of an early sanctuary area.

Markinch's railway station dates from 1847 and the Town Hall in

Betson Street from 1857; the core of the old town offers a range of mostly nineteenth-century buildings, although Galloway Inn, Kirk Street, is an eighteenth-century coaching inn. Within decades of modernity Markinch still struggles to retain an independent character in the shadow of the new town of Glenrothes. And, like many other Fife settlements, many new houses are being 'infilled' to open or derelict sites in the town centre.

METHIL

Today Methil, made a burgh of barony around 1665, is the centre part of the industrial sprawl from Leven in the east to Buckhaven in the west. Its engulfing began in the expansion of the late nineteenth century when the mining industry flourished. Before this Methil was also known for its salt manufacture. Mining has now ceased too, as the last coal shipment from Methil docks was loaded in 1970. Methil harbour and docks formed Fife's largest port, and began as a harbour built in 1661 by David, 2nd Earl of Wemyss, linked by a 1795 wagon-road to the mines at Buckhaven. The three docks evolved thus: No. 1, 1884–7; No. 2, 1894–1900; and No. 3, 1907–13. The local authority housing of 1919 onwards is still in place. Methil Church dates from 1924–5 and the influence of the Wemyss family is remembered particularly in the building known as the Randolph Wemyss Memorial Hospital of 1909.

METHILHILL

Now a western suburb of Methil, Methilhill evolved from the larger neighbouring mining community. The character of this colliers' quarter is refreshed by what is known as the 'garden-village miners' housing' of 1924–6 of the Wemyss Coal Co.

MIDDLE-FOODIE

(See also entry for Foodieash).
Note: Although Middle-Foodie is a place rather than even a hamlet, it is worthy of mention as it was once a portion of the medieval estate of Foodie.
Records show that in 1452 James II gave to James Kennedy, Bishop of St Andrews, the lands then described as 'Craigfudy, Mydelfudy

and Westerfudy'. Both the houses of today's Craigfoodie and Middle Foodie are of an eighteenth-century core with early nineteenth-century additions.

MILTON OF BALGONIE

Part of the old parish of Markinch, the village lies along the banks of the River Leven and evolved around a flax-spinning mill founded in 1807 and enlarged in the late 1830s; the mill closed in 1886 but gave its name to the 'Milton' derivation. The place was formerly known for its coal mining, iron (Leven Iron Co. 1802) and brickmaking.

The village retains a nucleus of nineteenth-century vernacular cottages, with a parish church of 1835–6. Milton House dates from 1770. The historic centrepiece of the area is the fifteenth-century Castle of Balgonie. Today the village is largely a dormitory of Glenrothes, Leven and Markinch.

(See also the entry for Coaltown of Balgonie.)

MONIMAIL

In medieval times Monimail – once written Money Meal – was within the property remit of the Archbishop of St Andrews. An episcopal tower-castle (Monimail Tower) was built here by Bishop William de Lamberton (d.1328), to be enlarged by Cardinal Beaton. Archbishop John Hamilton – the last medieval Archbishop of St Andrews – is known to have resided here and caused the planting of an orchard of French trees in the grounds; here too he entertained a youthful James V with hunting at Edinsmuir.

Monimail Tower is all that survives of a larger edifice overlooking the parish graveyard in which are buried the earls of Leven, Balfour and Melville. Monimail Church was built 1794–7, and its Gothic tower dates from 1811. Melville House at Monimail dates from 1692 and its garden houses from 1697.

Architectural historians aver that Melville House was the county's first mansion 'on a grandiose scale'. It was built for the 1st Earl of Melville by architect James Smith (c.1645–1731). Although trained in part for the priesthood, Smith was a colleague of Sir William Bruce, and in 1679 'married well', to the daughter of Robert Mylne, Master Mason to the Scottish Crown, succeeding Bruce as a surveyor of the king's works.

Monimail Tower

At Melville House estate is a pigeon-house or doocot (*c.* 1770), which, unusually, was converted from a windmill. It reminds us of how important pigeons were to Fife folk. Records show that Fife once had some 360 doocots with around 36,000 pairs of breeding pigeons, usually rock doves or rock pigeons. Although they were said to wreak 'dreadful havoc' in the Fife grain fields, purloining around 3,000–4,000 bolls (1 boll = 140 lbs) of grain a year, they were an important part of Fife estate economy. Doocots ensured a supply of fresh meat, eggs and fertiliser, particularly in the days before food preservation and the invention of the shotgun.

In Fife there are examples of cylindrical, turreted, horseshoe, conical and lectern doocots. In sixteenth-century Fife it was obligatory for landowners to build doocots; but only landowners, whether laird, prelate or minister, could do so. The job of pigeon-keeper was an important source of village employment up to the eighteenth century. It was a serious offence to break into a doocot. Ownership of a doocot appeared in the old description of an impoverished laird; he owned 'a puckle land, a lump of debt, a doocot and a law plea'.

NEWBURGH

The hamlet that was to develop into the town of Newburgh formed along one main street, travelling west of its source, the Tironesian Abbey of Lindores. The abbey had been founded in 1191 by David, Earl of Huntingdon, and was the central driving force of the area around until the abbey and precincts were sacked by the Reformers in 1543, and again in 1559 when the interior of the abbey church was desecrated and destroyed. The abbey was erected into a temporal lordship for Patrick Leslie, created Lord Lindores, by charter in 1600.

The monastic authorities founded a dependent *villam* at Newburgh before 1266, the year Alexander III elevated it to a burgh of barony with the right to hold a weekly market. In time these were joined by two annual fairs, known as the Race Fair and the Haggis Fair; the latter had been the Feast of St Katherine in medieval times and survived into the nineteenth century. By 1631 Charles I granted the settlement royal status (although it was never entered in the

James Stewart and Joseph Swan's engraving of Newburgh, 1840. Founded by the monks of the Order of Tiron at nearby Lindores Abbey, the place became a royal burgh in 1631. Fruit harvesting and salmon fishing was augmented by weaving which in turn gave way to linoleum manufacture. All these kept the quays of Newburgh busy. The spire of the Townhouse of 1808 is seen in the centre of the picture. [*Author's collection*]

Convention of Royal Burghs). Work at Newburgh became seasonal after the fall of the abbey which had supplied total employment; in the summer there was much salmon fishing and in the winter the weaving of linen dowlas cloth. The place was described by Cunningham in the seventeenth century as 'a poor country village'. By 1891 Newburgh was the centre of lino manufacure and its harbour ('The Shore') was a busy area for commercial and pleasure craft. The lino works closed in 1978. Apart from the abbey ruins the oldest buildings hereabouts are of the eighteenth and nineteenth centuries. The townhouse dates from 1808 and the parish church from 1905–06.

NEW GILSTON (see: BACKMUIR OF NEW GILSTON)

NEWPORT-ON-TAY

Few houses were built at Newport before the establishment of the modern ferry service to Dundee in 1822, and thereafter it became a popular area with the city's 'jute barons'. The first village of Newport was sustained by salmon fishing and a ferry was established here

Newport-on-Tay's original village was developed in Victorian times as a residential area for Dundee's 'jute barons'. It was once an important ferry terminal for Tay traffic. This print of around 1840 shows a paddle-steamer at the quay with Tayfield House, 1788, in the background; this was the home of the Berry family who had a hand in founding the ferry. [*Author's collection*]

from at least the twelfth century, possibly first administered by the monks of Arbroath Abbey on the site once known as Seamylnes. The ferry passed to private hands but by 1639 it was in municipal control. In the 1820s a new pier was constructed from the designs of Thomas Telford. The old ferry terminal is sited at Woodhaven. In time the greater portion of Newport was built on the Tayfield estate, which formed part of the old barony of Inverdovat. Tayfield House dates from 1788. Newport remains then as a Victorian development with a parish church of 1869–70 and is a commuter and retirement area.

NEWTON OF FALKLAND

The village appears in recorded history in July 1566 when Mary Queen of Scots granted to one Margaret Houseton and her son Thomas Beveridge quantities of barley from the village acres 'for her good service to the Queen at the birth of the prince of the realm'. The village was once known for its manufacture of dowlas and linen sheeting, and its maltings. There are extant eighteenth- and nineteenth-century properties and a disused industrial complex.

NORTH QUEENSFERRY

Today the village of North Queensferry, the first landfall encountered by medieval pilgrims on their way to the shrine of St Margaret at Dunfermline Abbey, is dominated by the road bridge of 1964 and the rail bridge of 1890. A royal ferry founded by Margaret, Saxon wife of Malcolm III, and the passage across the Forth was plied by passengers until 1964. North Queensferry was once a close-knit community centred on its now derelict piers. At the heart of the place is the now ruined St James' Chapel, Chapel Place, a fourteenth- and fifteenth- century foundation which historians say Robert the Bruce gave to the monks of Dunfermline Abbey. It was extensively damaged by Cromwell's troops in 1651. By the nineteenth century North Queensferry had developed as a fishing village and bathing resort, but is now a commuter habitation for Edinburgh. Extant buildings offer examples of eighteenth- and nineteenth-century construction.

The villages, hamlets, quays and havens of the Fife coast along from North Queensferry have long been a magnet and source of inspiration for painters, their canvases a rich source of detail on scenes of Fife life and character right up to the twenty-first century.

Sir David Wilkie's work in the genre is world famous but many lesser known artists like Charles Lees (1800–80) of Cupar are worthy of note showing how antique Fife village life might be assessed.

OAKLEY

Set along the A907 to Dunfermline, Oakley once had six blast furnaces for its flourishing Oakley Iron Works which started in 1846 but petered out by 1869. The village then evolved as a quiet mining settlement at the opening of the Blairhgall mine in 1911, and grew during the 1930s and 1940s after the sinking of the Comrie mine. Firm development was assured by the arrival of miners from the ailing Lanarkshire coalfields. By March 2002 all mining had ceased in Fife (with the closure of Longannet Mine, near Kincardine) and the village's mining character is now well and truly a relic part of Fife's industrial history.

OSNABURG (see: DAIRSIE)

PATHHEAD

Once called Dunnikier, from the estate on which it evolved, this village is in the ancient parish of Dysart and now effectively forms a part of the eastern suburbs of Kirkcaldy. It emerged in the sixteenth

Ravenscraig

century as a burgh of barony, and takes its name from the steep 'The Path'. Two houses are worthy of note: Path House (formerly Dunnikier House) was built by John Watson in 1692 and became the mansion of the Oswalds of Dunnikier; Hutchinson's House dates from 1793. The parish church dates from 1822–3, while Pathhead House is of 1882–4.

Although dominated by modern tower blocks, an important neighbour is Ravenscraig Castle above the cliffs of Pathhead sands. The castle was erected in 1460 as a marriage jointure of James II for his queen Mary of Guelders. In 1470 the castle – probably structually incomplete – was granted to William Sinclair, Earl of Caithness. To the east is Ravenscraig Park.

PEAT INN

Set along the B941 Cupar to Elie road, Peat Inn is within the district of Radernie and the old parish of Cameron. The hamlet's more modern history is associated with agriculture, but up to the late nineteenth century the surrounding acres were exploited for their coal resources. In medieval times it belonged to the Augustinian priory of St Andrews and was once rich in game; in 1645 the area was disjoined from St Andrews parish. Today the dwellings are largely nineteenth century.

PETTYCUR

An important ferry stop in former decades, with routes from it across the Forth to Leith and Newhaven for both commercial and passenger traffic. Roads out of Pettycur led north to the ferries of the Tay. It developed as an important watering-place known for its mineral well. Dr Anderson, physician to Charles I, did much to promote the efficacy of its waters. In history Pettycur is remembered as the place where Alexander III was killed in 1286 when his horse plunged over the cliffs while the king was on his way to Kinghorn Castle. The memorial stands to the tragedy on the A921 east of Kinghorn above Pettycur Bay Sands.

PICKLETILLEM

Neither a hamlet nor a village, Pickletillem is an area where a new Fife 'village' has developed from the late 1990s to cater for the interests of golf. Called Drumoig, the 'village' has a mixture of private residences, a hotel and golf courses.

PITLESSIE

Up to the fifteenth century the village of Pitlessie was in the owner-ship of the Ramorney family, and was sold in 1439 by Alexander de Ramorney to John, 1st Lord Lindsay of the Byres, to be further sold to the Crawfords of Mountquhanie in the reign of Charles II.

Once known for its maltings of 1890, now converted to private dwellings, the village was immortalised in Sir David Wilkie's *Pitlessie Fair* (1804), remembering a time when Pitlessie had two agricultural fairs per year. The site of the fairs was in the middle of Pitlessie near the house called 'Burnbrae' (once a public house). The dwellings today are mainly of the nineteenth century and the character is still rural.

PITSCOTTIE

The hamlet of Pitscottie, which was formed around the early 1800s, lies in what was the patrimonial estate of the vernacular prose historian Robert Lindsay (*c.* 1532–80), who wrote his credulous and picturesque *Historie and Chronicles of Scotland* covering the period 1436–1575. With its eighteenth-century bridge and a set on a main crossroads by the B940 from Cupar and the B939 from St Andrews, Pitscottie was an old posting station. There were two water-wheel mills here for spinning linen yarn, built in 1827 by J. and W. Yool.

PITTENWEEM

Pittenweem, within its eponymous old parish, was sustained in past decades by agriculture, fishing and handicrafts. The village core was made up of High Street, running east–west, with the sixteenth-century parish church (where the seventeenth-century tolbooth merges into its gable) at the east end, the Mid Shore and East Shore fronting the harbour, and the more modern James Street parallel with High Street and its extension into Marygate. The mercat cross stands by the old

Pittenweem

tolbooth and has the date 1711 on its capital, though its shaft may be of the sixteenth century.

The village that became Pittenweem owes its development to the priory of the Augustinian Canons. The acres that make up Pittenweem were first granted to the Benedictine monks of the Isle of May by David I around 1143, and were disponed to the Augustinians in the thirteenth century. The priory survived into the sixteenth century when it was transferred to the community of the burgh of Pittenweem by James VI in 1593; the priory lands were erected into a temporal lordship for Frederick Stewart in 1606. Thus the old fishing village of Pittenweem became a burgh of barony under the Augustinian priory, a burgh of regality in 1452, a royal burgh in 1541 and was enhanced by a grant of lands, harbour areas and so on by the priory in 1547.

Today Pittenweem remains a place of Flemish gables and designs and a flavour of old Pittenweem, when it was a fishing port trading with the Low Countries, can be seen in the Market Place and The Shore. Kellie Lodging, of around 1590, was the townhouse of the earls of Kellie and stands in restored form (1969–71) in High Street, and the Market Place affords buildings of the eighteenth and nine-

Pittenweem harbour was once a busy link for trade with the Low Countries;
the medieval village developed into a royal burgh by 1541. The parish church
of 1588 dominates the scene showing the seventeenth and eighteenth century
merchants dwellings of Mid and East Shore. [*Author's collection*]

teenth centuries. The oldest buildings are those which related to the
priory. Pittenweem harbour was in ruins by the sixteenth century,
but was repaired in 1687, and around it houses were established by
brewers, shipbuilders, fishermen, tobacco merchants and shipmasters. Most of the harbour house-facings today are of the nineteenth century.

RADERNIE

An old mining hamlet, which from 1645 was in the parish of
Cameron and formerly a part of heathland owned from the twelfth
century by the Augustinian priory of St Andrews. Now a scattering
of farms and dwellings south of Cameron Reservoir, Radernie has a
place in Fife's industrial history as one of the trio of collier settlements with Largoward and Lathones.

RATHILLET

The lands here were the property of the Crown until the reign of Malcolm IV, when they were chartered to Duncan, Earl of Fife, on his marriage to Ada, the king's neice. They were once again forfeit to the Crown and thereafter in the ownership of the Hackstones of Rathillet who held the property into the eighteenth century. Rathillet House dates from the 1790s.

ROTHES

For archaeologists Rothes is interesting as an area of Iron Age activity; there is a reconstructed souterrain (earth house) near Rothes House. Rothes is remembered in Fife's industrial history as a mining settlement: the Rothes Pithead Complex was built in 1947 and closed in 1961.

ST DAVID'S

Old seaport village on Inverkeithing Bay. St David's developed when in 1752 Sir Robert Henderson purchased land to build a harbour for the exporting of his coal from Fordell pits. The village further developed with the construction of salt pans. When the railway closed in 1946 St David's, which had once had its own customs house, ceased as a coal port. Thereafter the harbour and infrastructure went into decline, although shipbreaking was conducted in its environs. Today the village is being 'regenerated' with new housing developments as the 'St David's Harbour Village'.

ST MICHAEL'S

Set where the A92 and A 919 make a crossroads, this hamlet, by its eponymous wood and flanked by the Motray Water, still sports an inn whose former proprietor, one Michael, gave the place its name.

ST MONANS

St Monans (cf. St Monance – and pronounced locally as S'mi-nins) began as a small hamlet in a haven where the St Monance Burn meets the Forth. Here by the burn was situated the Shrine of St Monan, by today's kirk and graveyard, which gave the early hamlet its medieval pilgrim cachet.

St Monan, whose feast day was celebrated on 1 March in the pre-Reformation church, was an eighth-century cleric tutored by St Adrian, Bishop on the Isle of May, and became a missionary in Fife; records state that he was slain in a Viking raid. The pre-Reformation church of St Monans was founded by David II (r.1329–71) around 1369 on the site of a votive chapel; the new foundation was served by Dominican friars as chaplains and the construction of the new church was supervised by Sir William Dishington of nearby Ardross Castle. James III refounded the church in 1471; it survived until around 1557. It is likely that one of the Dominicans from the supporting convent (1476) in the shadow of the church served the shrine, which possibly contained corporeal relics of the saint. The pre-Reformation church was used as a parish church of the reformed faith after 1646; thereafter the congregation worshipped at Abercrombie Church. On the East Brae lay the chalybeate water Well of St Monan where pilgrims drank the supposedly curative waters and fishermen had their nets blessed.

In history St Monans was within the lands of Inverrin gifted by David I to the priory of the Isle of May. The superior of the land, Sir William Sandilands of nearby Newark Castle, granted a charter to St Monans in 1622. The harbour had an original pier of 1596, made into a central pier and flanked with east and west piers and breakwaters in 1865 and 1902. A Town Hall (once a school) dates from 1866. The oldest area, by the West, Mid and East Shore, where St Monans began, has buildings from the seventeenth to the nineteenth centuries. St Monans was an important fishing port from the fourteenth century.

About half a mile south of St Monans Church, on the cliffs overlooking Long Shank and Partan Craig, lie the ruins of Newark Castle. Originally in the possession of the Sandilands family, of whom James Sandilands of Cruive and St Monans made it a baronial seat in 1545, the castle had one distinguished owner. He was General David Leslie (d.1682), 1st Lord Newark, who defeated the Marquis of Montrose at the battle of Philiphaugh in 1645; later he changed sides and opposed Cromwell. Leslie's bones rested in the choir of St Monans kirk until 1828 when they were unceremoniously thrown over the sea wall by the zealous renovators. Newark passed to the Anstruthers and then the Bairds of Elie but has long been a lonely ruin; in 1898–9 the ruins were surveyed by Sir Robert Lorimer as a

The fourteenth-century parish church of St Monan at Braehead rises above the shore once busy with a hundred sail boats out of St Monans harbour. The village houses in this early Victorian print rise above the original pier of 1596 which was reconstructed in 1865 and 1902 to make a two-basin harbour. [*Author's collection*]

restoration plan for Sir William Burrell but the project was never taken up. The lands of Newark were to figure in an important industrial development which had important consequences for the Fifers who lived there.

Writing for the *Statistical Account* in 1790, the Rev. Archibald Gillies of St Monans parish had this to say:

> There is an abundance of coal in the lands of Newark, consisting of splint, cherry and culm, at present working. It is not level free, but wrought by a fire engine. Likewise one of the neatest and best contrived salt-works upon the coast, called St Philip's; both are the property of Sir John Anstruther, Baronet. The coal and salt, besides what is sold to the country, are exported at Pittenweem.

Here he gives evidence that the cliffs and shore between St Monans and Pittenweem were the location of a remarkable enterprise.

Sir John Anstruther (d.1799) inherited the estate of Newark in 1753 and supplied the capital to invest in 1771 in the Newark Coal and Salt Work Co. The colliery was located at the site of the extant Coal Farm, just north of a windmill; and nine salt pans were set out along the shore during 1772–4. Some fifty-six villagers from Wemyss to Dysart were employed at the colliery and salt pans. A wooden wagon-way for horse-drawn wagons was built from the mine and salt pans round to Pittenweem harbour at which Sir John Anstruther built a new central pier to ship the products of the enterprise. In passing it can be noted that for a good while before this Anstruther project was developed, coal was hewn here from the days when Oliver Cromwell's Ironsides galloped along these cliffs to subdue the coastal villages.

When the mine sustained a severe fire the wagon-way was abandoned (by 1794), but the colliery functioned at a much reduced capacity; mining stopped in 1813 and the salt pans were abandoned by 1823. Today the site has become an important relic of Fife's past industrial history for the eighteenth-century enterprise has not been obliterated by modern development; some of the wagon-way was reused when the coastal Leven and East Fife Railway line was developed in 1863–5. The last villager to work at the enterprise died in 1849. The reconstructed windmill remains as a landmark.

SALINE

A village described by John Leighton in 1840 as 'clean, and extremely picturesque', with 'houses neatly built and whitewashed' with kitchen gardens and flower beds. Saline is flanked by the Saline Hills in its eponymous parish. Once an agricultural community, this too was formerly a privately owned village. The settlement was long a royal 'gift' apportioned to that member of the royal family who held the title Earl of Mar. In spite of ironstone and coalmining activities Saline does retain some of the 'old-fashioned' charm with its eighteenth- and nineteenth-century dwellings. The present church was built in 1808–10 on a pre-Reformation site. Sir Walter Scott was a frequent visitor to Saline staying at eighteenth-century Nether Kinnedar with William Erskine, Lord Kinnedar of Session. Near to Saline are the ruins of seventeenth-century Killernie Castle, the centrepiece of an old estate that was in the hands of the Aytouns of Inchdairnie by the end of the nineteenth century.

SINCLAIRTOWN

The settlement now forms part of Kirkcaldy. This village developed from the 1750s on the estate of the earls of Rosslyn, and bears their family name St Clair. Pottery and linen weaving industries came and went, but in more recent times it was known for its ironworks, lino manufacturing and engineering shops. Hanklymuir Factory of 1860 is an architectural survivor. Viewforth Parish Church dates from 1875–57.

SPRINGFIELD

The village is set a mile or so back from the A92 Pitlessie–Cupar road, on land rising north from the River Eden. It retains the smallest railway station in Fife still open, although unmanned. The station house of 1847 is now a private dwelling. Local tradition has it that nearby Stratheden was a landlocked lake fed by numerous springs from which the village obtained its name; and in the sixteenth and seventeenth centuries there was extensive peat cutting in the area. Because of the nature of the ground, Springfield never had its own graveyard.

Down the ages Springfield has sported brick and tile works, jute and flax mills, quarries, sandpits and corn mills. Lack of industry caused Springfield's young folk to look elsewhere for work and the town of Waverley, South Dakota, USA, was founded by emigrants from Springfield. Springfield's church was built around 1861 and the church clock was set up in 1878. Around the 1850s the village had its own racecourse which became the factory area of Uthrogle Mills. To the north of the village lies Stratheden Hospital of around 1850 on the site of land known as the Retreat.

See: Entries for Crawford Priory, and Marie de Guise-Lorraine's encampment of 1559, and the Roman camp of Edenwood.

STAR OF MARKINCH

Star was once a weaving community and is set on an elevated position offering fine views of the Lomond Hills and the historic routes across Fife. It contains a variety of whinstone and pantiled cottages, with a range of modern dwellings. The old schoolhouse was the home of the Scottish novelist Annie S. Swan (1859–1943); she lived here when her husband Dr James Burnett Smith was school-master. A primary school was located here in 1815 with late nineteenth-century additions.

Note: Not to be confused with Starr, Kilmany, once a Crown estate in the portion of the earls of Fife. In 1527 James V conferred the lands on David Balfour of Burleigh; the Balfours held the lands until 1665.

STRATHKINNESS

Set on a hill with stupendous panoramic views at its northern elevation towards St Andrews Bay, the estuary of the River Eden, Tentsmuir Forest and beyond, Strathkinness tumbles south down the hill towards the Kinness Burn as it makes its final meander to the sea at the East Sands, St Andrews.

The village first appears on record in 1144 when Bishop Robert of St Andrews gave the lands to the Augustinian priory of St Andrews and a settlement was established by 1160 nearer to the B939 than the modern village. After the Reformation the lands fell to the Balfours of Burleigh and they were forfeit to the Crown because the Jacobite Balfours were involved in the 1715 rebellion. The policies were purchased by the Melville family in 1724 and so remained until 1900 when they were sold to James Younger of Alloa. The Youngers built Mount Melville mansion house (1903) and in 1947 the grounds of the house were sold to the then Fife County Council. The mansion was used first as a maternity hospital, then as a geriatric hospital and is now a golfing complex. Thus Strathkinness lay between medieval roads leading to St Andrews and was an agricultural community with a considerable amount of weaving in the eighteenth and nine-teenth centuries. Quarrying was also an important local industry up to modern times. A Free Church was established in Strathkinness in 1843 and the much altered church of 1867 is now the village hall. The parish church dates from 1864 and has also been greatly altered; the manse of 1873 is now a private house.

STRATHMIGLO

Set at the western extremity of the How of Fife, on the River Eden, Strathmiglo gives its name to the old parish and the former name of the Eden at this point, the Miglo and its strath (rural valley). In early medieval times the lands of Strathmiglo were Crown property

This turn-of-the-nineteenth-century photograph of Strathmiglo's main street shows the Town Hall steeple of 1734. The building offers a fine example of the typical heart of a Fife village, wherein the town's lockup and civic centre were all of a piece. Strathmiglo became a burgh of barony in the sixteenth century and was a centre of hand- then, power-loom weaving. [*Staralp*]

granted to Duncan, Earl of Fife, by Malcolm IV in 1160, on his marriage to the king's neice Ada; the lands remained in the Earldom until 1424, with the Scotts of Balwearie as tenants from 1251.

Historically, too, Strathmiglo had some interestingly named suburbs: Kirklands, where the provost and prebendaries lived; Stedmoreland, held by the abbey of Balmerino and forfeit to the Crown in 1746; Temple, once owned by the Knights Templar and then the Knights of St John of Jerusalem. There were feus named Wester Cash and Town.

Sir William Scott of Balwearie was to be an important heritor. He was present at the Battle of Flodden in 1513, taken prisoner and ransomed through the sale of Strathmiglo properties, becoming an occasional Commissioner of the Scottish Parliament; he died around 1532. Sir William obtained a charter from James IV to form Strathmiglo into a barony, with powers to elevate the village into a burgh of barony; the latter only came into effect in 1600 at the instance of Sir James Scott. All of this was confirmed by James VI in 1605. Strathmiglo was known for its weekly Friday market and its fairs of St Cyralus (9 June), St Crispin (25 October) and St Martin (November). Around 1730 superiority of the village was passed to the Balfours of Burleigh.

In 1734 a steeple was built alongside the extant tolbooth from stone from Strathmiglo Castle at Wester Strathmiglo. The castle earned the nickname of 'Cairney-flappit' because of its hurried erection. The medieval church of St Martin at Strathmiglo was served by the clergy of the bishopric of Dunkeld and had its own pedagogy to supply education for those who were to enter church service. The present church was erected 1783–4. The parish once boasted five schools.

TAYPORT

Once called Ferry-Port-On-Craig, from the old parish name of 1606, Tayport derives its historical importance as a ferry port for vessels plying across the Tay to Broughty Ferry and the hinterland of Angus. It was created a burgh of barony by the 1598 charter of James VI in favour of Robert Durie of that Ilk. Ferry trade declined after the opening of the ferry to Newport, nevertheless Tayport retained importance as a quay to discharge cargoes of coal, lime and so on, and load grain, potatoes and other produce from North Fife into the twentieth century. The arrival of the railway in 1842 prompted the

Edinburgh and Northern Railway Co. to buy ferry rights in 1846 and Tayport harbour was developed to accommodate the huge iron paddlesteamers fitted with rails for the carrying of loaded coal trucks across the Tay. A new harbour was constructed in 1851.

The village once supported an annual fair, the survivor of a medieval market, and the old mercat cross is preserved at Dalgleish Street; this street and Tay Street contained the early core of the village. Tayport has been known by that name since 1846 and the Victorian village had a sawmill (1850), a spinning works (1864) and an engineering works (1875). The truck ferry closed when the second railway bridge across the Tay was opened in 1887, but a passenger ferry remained; the ferryboat service ceased to run in 1939, and Tayport station closed to passengers in 1966.

By the twelfth century a hospice and chapel for travellers was built here, both run by the monks of Arbroath Abbey, and by 1607 the old parish church was *in situ* in Castle Street; it was restored in 1794 and 1825. The church spire still leans towards the church because of a weakness in the Scotscraig vault below. Its graveyard marks the passing of the old village folk, from the handloom weavers and the jute spinners to the salmon fishers and the shipbuilders. As the fifteenth century developed, the ferry crossing to Angus was deemed to be of such strategic importance to warrant a castle for protection. In 1855 only fragments of the castle remained and were demolished to make way for the rapidly expanding burgh; the site of the castle is the dwelling Castle Cottage, in Castle Street.

The estate of Scotscraig, above where the village of Tayport developed, was established by the twelfth century and belonged to the See of St Andrews which feued it in the reign of Alexander III to Sir Michael Scott of Balwearie. By 1652 the estate was in the hands of the Erskines who extended their ownership to the whole of Tayport, its ferry and surrounding corn mill, brewery and fisheries. In the reign of Charles II the whole estate became the property of the murdered Archbishop James Sharp. The Dalgleishes built the present mansion of 1807, Scotscraig Mains in 1821 and the road to Newport in 1830. Another owner, Vice Admiral W. H. Maitland-Dougall, acquired the estate in 1845 and was responsible for setting up the present Scotscraig Golf Club (founded in 1817 and re-established 1887). Tayport's disused East Lighthouse was built by Robert Stevenson in 1832, the year he also designed the West Lighthouse. The stilted box Pile Lighthouse (c.1848) still exists.

A neighbour of Tayport is Tentsmuir Forest, once the habitation of shipwrecked mariners, vagabonds and outlaws, who hid among the trees, scrub and midden mounds formerly the home of Stone Age and Bronze Age people. Now the area is the home of important Nature Reserves at Morton Lochs and Tentsmuir Point. The medieval chroniclers filled the dunes and groves with *diaboli, ursus et bos primiginius*, devils, bear and oxen, which gives a clue to one animal very important in Fife village life.

Wild oxen were once native to Fife, but it was probably the monastic agriculturalists who introduced oxen to the village economy. The monastic acres were cultivated with eight or twelve team ox ploughs. In time such great ploughs and their ox teams were owned in common by villages. Such a plough is mentioned in the old poem 'The Wyf of Auchtermuchty' (*Bannatyne Manuscript*, 1568) wherein 'Sche lowsit oxen aucht or nine'.

THORNTON

The village of Thornton, by the River Ore, enters history as an important railway junction and was dubbed the centre of the East Fife coalfields. The Rothes pit that offered Thornton prosperity has been long closed. Before this Thornton was once a noted staging village with famous hostelries like Beach Inn and Strephan's Inn; a bypass was opened in 1983. The parish church dates from 1834–5. The nearby Town Clock, set in its distinctive black and white turret, was a gift of Waldegrave Leslie of Leslie House, to mark Queen Victoria's Jubilee of 1897. The primary school in Station Road dates from 1904.

TORRYBURN

The rural village aspects of Torryburn suffered much from the nineteenth-century expansion of the coal trade. Nevertheless the mansion house and lands of Torry belonged to the Wardlaws, whose scion Henry Wardlaw became Bishop of St Andrews (1404–40) and Cardinal Walter Wardlaw, Bishop of Glasgow (1367–89). At Torryburn was set a harbour for Dunfermline goods to be shipped to Barrowstouness and thence to London. In the eighteenth century Torryburn was also known for its weaving as well as mining. Torryburn Parish Church dates from 1800 and the area still sports cottages of the eighteenth and nineteenth century. Torryburn is also associated with the other settlements along the Forth shore of Low Torry and Newmills where there was once the monastic *Novum Molendinium*.

TOWNHILL

A former collier village now merged with Dunfermline's ever expanding northeastern suburbs. Townhill's former public library and baths of 1905–06 became a community centre. The primary school dates from 1875.

VALLEYFIELD (see: LOW VALLEYFIELD)

WEST WEMYSS

Lying along the shores of the Forth, West Wemyss once depended upon salt panning and the coal industry for its prosperity. The village grew up as a consequence of Wemyss Castle and estate, which belonged to the ancient Scottish family of the same name. The local folk once referred to the sixteenth-century port and village of West Wemyss as the 'Haven Town of Wemyss' and were proud of its status as a burgh of barony, granted by James IV in 1511. West Wemyss' tolbooth 'for the cribbing of vice and service to crown' was built by

Wemyss Castle

Made a burgh of barony in 1511, West Wemyss was a thriving centre for the salt-panning industry then a busy coal port. The harbour was founded by David Wemyss around 1512 to facilitate Wemyss Castle. [*Author's collection*]

David, 4th Earl of Wemyss (1678–1720). Around the middle of the twentieth century the place was run down but since 1987 the inner sixteenth-century harbour has been filled in and the surrounding seventeenth- and nineteenth-century buildings renovated. St Adrian's Parish Church dates from 1890–95, and the primary school from 1896.

The earliest parts of Wemyss Castle date from the fifteenth century, but it has been added to many times.

WINDYGATES AND CAMERON BRIDGE

Windygates was once bisected by the stagecoach routes between north and central Fife and the ferries on the south shore of the county. Posting was its principal industry.

Cameron Bridge, across the River Leven, replaces one which tradition dates from 1532, built at the instigation of Cardinal David Beaton. Formerly, the settlement of Cameron Bridge was a place of spinners and bleachers. Cameron Hospital, opened as a fever hospital in 1911, takes in the grounds of the old mansion of Cameron Bridge House of 1849. The distillery which James Haig acquired from Eddington of West Wemyss in 1818 was on this site.

WORMIT

Wormit owes its existence to the Tay Railway Bridge which dominates the area here. There was a tiny hamlet around Scroggie-side Farm before the site was chosen as the Fife terminus of the bridge. It is said that Wormit was the first village in Scotland to have electric light, a facility introduced by one Alexander Stewart who built many of the Victorian houses here; power was generated by a windmill on Wormit Hill supplemented by a steam engine which gave way to a coal-gas engine which chugged away until 1930. Wormit Station was opened in 1889 but was closed to passengers in 1969. The village has largely become a dormitory for Dundee. Wormit Parish Church dates from 1898–1901.

APPENDIX I
VILLAGE SAINTS

The formal and public recognition of exemplary sanctity as we now know it is attached to papal recognition. Yet for a long time the people of medieval Fife chose, usually, churchmen by popular acclaim or local cult to act on their behalf as mediators in prayer. For instance, and before the Reformation, several Fife villages chose certain saints to be their patrons; often Celtic saints were chosen who were not a part of the central prayer of the Mass called the Canon. To underline their devotion by villagers, saints were depicted on churches, priories, abbeys and cathedral bosses, brasses, misericords, screens, glass, sculpture, coats of arms, seals and a variety of public buildings – all to bring the protection and benediction of the saints so featured.

Fife abbeys and priories had their own dedications, like the Tironesian abbey at Lindores which went for 'a full house' of patronage from the Blessed Virgin, St Andrew the Apostle and All Saints. Fife's medieval guildsmen also chose saints to be their patrons from St Eligius, patron of saddlers, watchmakers, goldsmiths, blacksmiths, cutlers and pewterers, to St Martin of Tours, patron of knights and tailors, who with St Thomas Becket of Canterbury was a popular saint in medieval Fife. Sometimes these church and guild saints were acclaimed by local folk outside their particular remit, for Fife villagers being independent folk chose their own patrons irrespective of any other local ties. Here are some examples of saints particularly associated with Fife villages:

ADAMNAN. *c.* 625–704. 9th Abbot of Iona. Biographer of St Columba. Celtic saint. Feast: 23 September. Particular patronage: INCHKEITH.

ADRIAN or MAGRIDIN. d.*c.*875. Missionary bishop of the Isle of May. Martyred by Danes. Feast: 4 March. Particular patronage: ISLE OF MAY; LINDORES; FLISK; parish of ABDIE. Note: The old Burgh Seal of PITTENWEEM is deemed to show the figure of St Adrian in full canonicals aboard a barque; this blazon of arms was prepared in 1676 by Sir Charles Erskine, Lyon King of Arms.

ANDREW. 1st century. Apostle and martyr. Patron saint of Scotland. Shrine at St Andrews Cathedral. Feast: 30 November. Particular patronage: many important sites in Fife associated with him, for instance in 1456 the magistrates and council at St Andrews set up and endowed an altar to the Apostle at Holy Trinity Church. Conjoined with St Fillan at FORGAN.

CAINNECH or **KENNETH**. Irish cleric. Also known as Kenneth of Achabo, arrived at Kilrymont (ST ANDREWS) in 570. Left Fife 578. Particular patronage: KENNOWAY.

COLUMBA. *c.* 521–97. Began missionary work at Iona in 563. Relics at Dunkeld by 815, transferred there by Constantine, King of the Picts. Feast: 9 June. Altar patronised by provost and magistrates of St Andrews at Holy Trinity Church. Particular patronage: EMONIA; COLM'S INCH; INCHCOLM.

ETHERNAN. Irish cleric. Bishop. Evangelist of the Scots. Feast: 3 December. Chapel on the ISLE OF MAY. Particular patronage: KILRENNY; LATHRISK.

ETHERNASC or **ATHERNASE**. In 1244 David de Bernham, Bishop of St Andrews, rededicated Leuchars Church to this shadowy saint. Particular patronage: LEUCHARS; LATHRISK.

FILLAN. Eighth-century Scoto-Irish missionary. Reliquary arm of St Fillan was carried into battle at Bannockburn in the care of Maurice, Abbot of Inchaffray. Feast: 9 January. Cave and well at PITTENWEEM. Legendary 'Abbot of Pittenweem'. Particular patronage: ABERDOUR; FORGAN.

KENTIGERN or **MUNGO**. d. 603. Apostle of Cumbria. Feast: 13 January. A legend, backed by the *Vita S.Kentigerni*, links Kentigern with Fife thus: St Kentigern's mother was Thenew, daughter of Loth, King of Lothian. She became pregnant (some say by Prince Ewan) but refused to marry the father; humiliated Loth ordered that she be set adrift in a leather coracle at the mouth of the Aberlessie (Aberlady) stream. A divine hand, says the legend, caused her coracle to beach safely where Culross now stands. She gave birth at this place where St Serf had founded a religious house and the child was succoured here. Particular patronage: CULROSS.

MAELRUBHA. d. *c.*724. Irish religious, migrated to Iona. Feast: 21 April. Chapel of Crail castle dedicated to this saint. Particular patronage: CRAIL.

MEMMA. In 1234 David de Bernham rededicated the church at Scoonie to St Memma (or Memme) the Virgin. Particular patronage: SCOONIE.

MODRUST or **DROSTAN.** d.*c.* 610. Irish. A monk in the tutorship of St Columba. First Abbot of Deer, Aberdeenshire. Venerated as one of the Apostles of Scotland. When David de Bernham, Bishop of St Andrews, was undertaking his massive church rededication programme he rededicated the church at Markinch to St John the Baptist in 1234. It seems that the villagers of the day did not forsake their saint and St Drostan was ever associated with their parish. Particular patronage: MARKINCH; ABERDOUR (where a holy well was dedicated in his name).

MONAN. d. 874. A trainee of St Adrian; missionary in the Firth of Forth lands. Slain by the Danes. Feast: 1 March. Particular patronage: ST MONANS; KILCONQUHAR.

NINIAN. d.*c.*432. Established a mission at *Candida Casa* (Whithorn). Evangelised the Britons and Picts. Feast: 26 August. His biographer Adamnan speaks of a chapel or cell dedicated to him at INCHKEITH. A chapel to him was sited at DUNFERMLINE (between High St and West Queen Anne St), founded by John Christison, Vicar of CREICH. Particular patronage: ABBOTS-HALL parish; ABDIE parish; FALKLAND; CERES.

REGULUS or **RULE.** *c.* Fourth century. Prime character in the story of the translation of the corporeal relics of Andrew, apostle and martyr, from Constantinople to the Pictish enclave which developed as ST ANDREWS. His cave (now vanished in cliff erosion) long pointed out at St Andrews. Feast: 17 October. Particular patronage: ST ANDREWS.

SERF or SERVANUS. Contradictory stories or legends about him. Probably a contemporary of Adamnan. Known as apostle to West Fife. Adoptive father of St Kentigern. Cave at Dysart. Founded church at Culross where he died and was buried. Feast: 1 July. For decades the people of Culross had a special procession in his honour on this day, whereat they paraded carrying green boughs. A chaplaincy was set up by Laurence of Lindores in 1434 at Holy Trinity Church, St Andrews. Particular patronage: CREICH; CULROSS; DYSART; BURNTISLAND. A number of old Fife charters note that the following gave Fife lands, with their settlements, in his name to endow the church: Macbeth and Queen Gruoch gave BOGIE, near Kirkcaldy; Malcolm III (Canmore) and Queen Margaret gave BALCHRISTIE; while the last Celtic Bishops of St Andrews, Maeldirin, Tuthald and Fothad II, High Bishop of Alban, added MARKINCH, SCOONIE and AUCHTERDERRAN. In passing too, it can be added that Andrew Wyntoun (c1. 355–1422), historian and Prior of St Serf's, Lochleven, wrote that Serf once had a tussle with the Devil himself at DYSART and banished him from Fife:

> Then saw the Dewyl that he cowthe noucht
> With all the wylis that he sowcht
> Ourecum Saynct Serf ...

FIFE VILLAGE PILGRIMAGE ROUTES

Because of the two great shrines at Dunfermline (St Margaret) and St Andrews (St Andrew the Apostle and Martyr), Fife was a magnet for pilgrims; there were also relics to visit of St Ethernan at the Isle of May and at the Columban shrine at Emonia (Inchcolm). At certain feasts of the church – not just 'When the sweet showers of April fall and shoot' as identified by Geoffrey Chaucer – Fife village folk joined the far-travelled pilgrims down the five pilgrim routes across Fife:

1. EARLSFERRY TO ST ANDREWS via Kilconquhar, Largoward and Lathockar.
2. KIRKCALDY TO ST ANDREWS via Kennoway and the 'Pilgrim's Gait' to Ceres, Pitscottie and the Bishop's Road to Blebo and Magus Muir.
3. QUEENSFERRY TO DUNFERMLINE THEN ST ANDREWS, first via Queen Margaret's ferry across the Forth to Dunfermline,

then north to Scotlandwell and the hospice of St Mary to Markinch, Kennoway and beyond.

4. TAYPORT TO ST ANDREWS via Leuchars and Guardbridge where there was a *statio*, where pilgrims met, often to be taken under guard through the wild places of Kincaple to St Andrews Cathedral.

5. WEST FIFE TO ST ANDREWS via Newburgh, the Abbey of Lindores, and maybe the Abbey of Balmerino to Cupar, Dairsie and beyond. This route offered a number of options: pilgrims could visit the Grange of Lindores, the abbey granaries, the church of Holy Trinity, Moonzie, and maybe the Preceptory of Dunbog. One established route also bypassed Cupar to pass Pitbladdo and Foodieash to Dairsie and Guardbridge.

Each route passed through Fife hamlets, villages, abbey and priory lands and towns where a medieval infrastructure supplied food, shelter and entertainment at village inns and monastic hospices. Time, agriculture, the Reformation and building projects have altered the pilgrim landscape of Fife where routes were clearly marked by boundary crosses and wayside shrines. Nevertheless pilgrims were once an important part of Fife villages' economies and made the place as famous in medieval Europe as the routes from the shrine of St James at Compostela in Spain to Rome itself.

APPENDIX II
VILLAGES WITH FORMER RAILWAY LINKS

Village folk in Fife were first introduced to the concept of railways in 1840, a time when the county had no bridge links with Angus–Dundee or Lothian–Edinburgh. By 1845 no less than sixteen railway projects were mooted for Fife as railway mania gripped the nation.

TIMESCALE

*c.*1770 Fordell Railway, for coal workings, ran from CROSSGATES to ST DAVID'S HARBOUR. Survived until 1946.

1768 Earl of Elgin's Railway, LIMEKILNS to CHARLESTOWN. Bought by the North British Railway in 1862. Passenger traffic, 1894.

1783 Halbeath Railway used horse haulage to take coal to INVER-KEITHING. Survived until 1867.

1847 Edinburgh and Northern Railway first forged track through Fife. Line ran from BURNTISLAND to TAYPORT.

1849 Edinburgh and Northern Railway became Edinburgh, Perth and Dundee Railway.

1862 Edinburgh, Perth and Dundee Railway taken over by the North British Railway. Fife covered by tracks including Fife and Kinross, Kinrosshire, Leven and East Fife and St Andrews, Stirling and Dunfermline, West Fife Mineral.

1879 28 December, Tay Railway Bridge Disaster.

1887 New railway bridge erected over the Tay.

1890 Forth Railway Bridge opened.

1923 Railways grouped into London and North Eastern Railway.

1948 Nationalisation of railways became part of British Railways. Extant Fife railways became part of Scottish Region.

1963 Beeching Report sealed fate of many rural lines in Fife.

1967 Steam-hauled locomotives disappeared from Fife lines. Opening of Lochty private railway. Closed and dismantled in 1990s.

1970 Wemyss Private Railway, connecting collieries with METHIL docks closed.

ANSTRUTHER. Anstruther to Kilconquhar, September 1863. First station closed 1 September 1883. Last passenger train covered East

Coast Line, 25 June 1966.

AUCHTERMUCHTY. Opened 1857; closed to passengers 1950; line abandoned 1964.

BOARHILLS. To Anstruther, September 1883; to St Andrews, June 1887. Closed, 22 September 1930, freight continued to October 1964. Dwelling now replaces station house.

BUCKHAVEN. Closed 10 January 1955.

BURNTISLAND. September 1847 a line was developed to Cupar.

CAIRNEYHILL. Line closed 7 July 1930.

CAMERON BRIDGE. Closed 6 October 1969.

CHARLESTOWN. A wagon-way here for coal mines. Line rebuilt and passenger services opened 1 September 1894. Closed to passengers 1926.

COLLESSIE. Closed 19 September 1955.

COWDENBEATH. Fife and Kinross Railway. Mawcarse to Cowdenbeath opened June 1860. Old station closed 31 March 1919.

CRAIL. East Fife Coast Line. Crail to St Andrews closed to freight 5 October 1964. Closed 6 September 1965. Site of station now garden centre.

CROSSGATES. Closed 26 September 1949.

CULROSS. July 1906 a line built to Dunfermline. Closed 7 July 1930. Line remained open for trans-shipment of coal.

CUPAR. Opened 17 May 1848.

DAIRSIE. Closed 20 September 1954.

DALGETY BAY. Station opened 1997.

DYSART. Opened 1847, closed 1969.

ELIE. 1862. Closed 6 September 1965. Housing estate now covers site.

GATESIDE. Line abandoned 1964.

GLENROTHES WITH THORNTON. Station opened 1992.

GUARDBRIDGE. Station closed 6 September 1965; freight to St Andrews closed 20 June 1966. Line built over, bridge demolished (piers remain).

HALBEATH. Horse haulage wagon-way 1783–1867. Coal to Inverkeithing. Closed 22 September 1930.

INVERKEITHING. North Junction–East Junction. Service withdrawn, 24 November 1989.

KELTY. Closed 22 September 1930.

KENNOWAY. Goods sidings closed August 1964.

KILCONQUHAR. Line to Anstruther 1863; closed 6 September 1965.

KILMANY. Closed 12 February 1951.

KINGSBARNS. Closed 22 September 1930.

LADYBANK. Bridge of Earn to Ladybank, opened 18 July 1845; link with Perth opened July 1848; Mawcarse to Ladybank closed May 1962; Bridge of Earn to Ladybank re-established 1975.

LARGO. 1863. Closed 6 September 1965.

LARGOWARD. Goods station. Closed 1964.

LESLIE. Branch line 1857. Station closed 1932. Goods only until October 1967. Leven to Thornton, 3 July 1854.

LEUCHARS. Old station closed 3 October 1921; Leuchars Junction closed 1 June 1878 when a more direct route to Dundee was opened. Leuchars to Tayport service closed 9 January 1956.

LEVEN. First station closed, 1 June 1867. Line opened (to Kilconquhar) July 1857. Leven to St Andrews closed September 1965; closed 6 October 1969.

LINDORES. First station opened 17 May 1848; closed 12 February 1951.

LOCHTY. Goods line of the North British Railway, 1898. Route of the East Fife Central Railway for coal and farm produce. Closed August 1964. Lochty Private Railway started June 1967. Small platform built at Knightsward. Line closed and lifted in the late 1990s.

LUNDIN LINKS. 1863. Closed 6 September 1965.

LUTHRIE. Closed 12 February 1951.

METHIL. North British Railway bought private railway and Methil docks in 1889. Link to Thornton South Junction. Station closed 10 January 1955; freight continued to 1965.

MONTRAVE. Opened 1898. Goods station. Closed August 1964.

MOUNT MELVILLE. Closed 22 September 1930.

NEWBURGH. Newburgh to Glenburnie Station, opened 1909; branch to St Fort; closed 19 September 1955; through trains from 1975.

NEWPORT ON TAY. Had East and West stations, both closed 5 May 1969; branch to TAYPORT closed 23 May 1966.

OAKLEY. Closed 7 October 1968.

PITTENWEEM. 1863. Closed 6 September 1965.

ROSYTH. Passengers and freight to dockyard. Station closed 24 November 1989. (Line built during the First World War by Admiralty and opened 1915.)

ST MONANS.   1863. Closed 6 September 1965.
STRATHMIGLO.   Line abandoned 1964.
STRAVITHIE.   Closed 22 September 1930.
TAY PORT (FERRY-PORT-ON-CRAIG).   First opened 17 May
    1848. Train ferry inaugurated 1 July 1852. Closed 12 May 1879.
TAYPORT.   Line to LEUCHARS closed 9 January 1956. Closed
    to NEWPORT-ON-TAY (EAST), 22 May 1966.
THORNTON (JUNCTION).   Opened 1848. Railway crossroads
    of Fife. Closed 1969.
TORRYBURN.   Line closed 7 July 1930.
WEMYSS (WEST).   1881. Opening of Wemyss and Buckhaven
    railway. Closed 17 November 1949.
WEMYSS CASTLE.   Closed 10 January 1955.
WORMIT.   Operating to Leuchars in 1879, also Newport-on-Tay
    and Tayport. Closed 5 May 1969.

Note: Stations still operating:
ABERDOUR
BURNTISLAND
COWDENBEATH LOOP TO DUNFERMLINE
CUPAR
DUNFERMLINE LOOP TO INVERKEITHING
INVERKEITHING
KINGHORN
KIRKCALDY
LADYBANK
LEUCHARS
MARKINCH
SPRINGFIELD
QUEENSFERRY, NORTH

Closed stations on extant main line, Edinburgh to Aberdeen:
DAIRSIE, 1954
DONIBRISTLE HALT, 1959
DYSART, 1969
FALKLAND ROAD, 1958
KINGSKETTLE, 1967
ST FORT, 1965
SINCLAIRTOWN, 1969
THORNTON JUNCTION, 1969